ALL OUT!

THE SAFEST
WAY TO LIVE

DAN HOOPER

ALL OUT!

Copyright © 2005 by Dan Hooper

ISBN: 0-9755311-4-X

Published by

LifeBridge
Books
P.O. BOX 49428
CHARLOTTE, NC 28277

Printed in the United States of America.

DEDICATION

To my wife and life partner,
Anna, whose love for me continues to ignite
enthusiasm, passion and creativity.
I love being with you.

CONTENTS

INTRODUCTION

Chuck Yeager, the legendary test pilot, became known as the "fastest man alive" when he was the first to fly a plane faster than the speed of sound.

The media, enthralled with the event, talked endlessly about the marvels of technology. Yeager, however, said, "It's the man, not the machine!"

From the beginning, the Creator gave His children dominion over this earth and He is not looking for average or mediocre performance. God expects us to learn His principles and make a personal decision to be fully committed—mentally, physically and spiritually.

The book you are about to read is not about theories or ideas, it's about YOU, and tells step-by-step how you can begin to live life to its fullest.

YOUR HIDDEN RESOURCES

I am totally convinced there is untapped potential within you—hidden resources that, when released, will give you incredible new meaning. Even more, the same God who endows you with creativity, will empower you with strength and vitality necessary to complete any task.

From personal experience, counseling others and divine principles, I want to share what I have discovered concerning the power of confession and vow-making, the necessity of a covenant relationship and how to find your personal assignment from heaven.

We'll also discuss becoming a rock-solid person—the YOU God is searching for.

IT'S TIME FOR ANSWERS

If you are ready to say farewell to a dull, ordinary life, read on.

You'll find answers to these questions:

– What are the dangers of playing it safe?
– How can I take charge of my emotions—
   instead of having my feelings control me?
– Why do people self-sabotage their success,
   and how can it be avoided?
– What does God's Word say concerning inner
   strength, commitment and perseverance?
– What is the secret of making resolutions that
   last?
– How can I maintain a full-speed-ahead life
   without tension and stress?
– Is there a way I can sustain my energy and
   enthusiasm?

Vince Lombardi once said, "A man's finest hour is when he has worked his heart out in a good cause and lies exhausted on the field of battle—victorious!"

It is my prayer this book will inspire a God-given vision and provide you with the "right stuff" to live the *all out* life.

– Dan Hooper

CHAPTER 1

ALL OUT?
OR PLAYING
IT SAFE?

It was a picture-perfect setting, a beautiful July afternoon in Grand Junction, Colorado. My brother and his 18-year old son were visiting from Florida, where my brother is a pastor.

I couldn't wait to show them the western slope of the Rocky Mountains—and to make them jealous of the cooler climate we enjoy in this part of the world. We headed for an area on the Grand Mesa known as Thunder Mountain, renting three All Terrain Vehicles to explore this gorgeous territory, home to porcupines, mountain lions, coyotes, red fox, elk and deer.

On this playground in the sky (elevation 9,100 feet), the clear running streams are dotted with beaver-dammed ponds—stocked with trout. Regal aspen trees line every trail.

After a picnic lunch, some unsuccessful fishing and friendly chatter over why anyone would choose to live in Florida rather than Colorado, it was time to start down the mountain. After loading up, the last words of advice this big brother gave were, "Be careful on these narrow trails. You never know what's coming around the next corner!"

THE DUST WENT FLYING!

Not heeding my own advice, I took off first and decided to keep the lead—having no intention of eating dirt behind a couple of Florida flat-landers.

This was no leisurely downhill sightseeing tour. I pushed the accelerator all the way, stuck it in fifth gear and zoomed off like a teenager. The dust went flying and I was barely hanging on—with my brother and nephew close behind. This was big time fun and I was relishing every moment!

Fish-tailing every turn and bend on the tight trail made it almost impossible to see what might be coming toward us. At one point I thought, "This path had better be clear of any animals or vehicles."

The three ATVs loaded with fishing and camping gear coming toward us had no idea what lay ahead.

I made a new friend that day—a retired plumber who

was on his way to a high mountain lake to fish for rainbow trout. We met head on—and thankfully damaged our ATVs far worse than our bodies.

My full-throttle downhill ride ended with an ambulance ride to the hospital, surgery on my wrist, six months of rehabilitation and a much higher golf score!

CHARGED UP—TURNED ON!

As I learned first hand, being totally committed to *anything* means risk—whether starting a new business, entering a personal relationship or even riding down a mountain path. It can be exhilarating, frightening, and often dangerous.

Sometimes we risk our heart, but this time it was our limbs.

You may say, "Wait just a minute, Dan. Why would I want to read this book if the results might put my life in jeopardy?"

Let me assure you, what you are about to discover does not concern foolish decisions. I want

> I WANT TO OPEN THE DOOR FOR YOU TO LIVE A CHARGED-UP, TURNED-ON, EXCITING LIFE.

to open the door for you to live a charged-up, turned-on, exciting life—one which revolutionizes your mind, heart and soul. It will make any temporary setbacks or mistakes pale in comparison.

You'll see how this full-sails-ahead lifestyle impacts

everything, including your relationship to God.

STAY OUT OF THE MIDDLE!

We all have two choices: we can either play it safe or be fully committed, venturing outside our comfort zone. Trying to waffle between the two is a recipe for disaster.

As Texan Jim Hightower puts it: "There's nothing in the middle of the road but yellow stripes and dead armadillos."

———◆———

WE CAN EITHER PLAY IT SAFE OR BE FULLY COMMITTED, VENTURING OUTSIDE OUR COMFORT ZONE.

Let's look at a few characters in the Bible who were confronted with difficult choices, yet made the right decisions.

Noah didn't play it safe.

When God told Noah to build an ark to save his family and all living creatures, he could have argued and complained, No way! I'll be a laughingstock around here!"

After all, these people had never *ever* seen rain. But Noah walked with the Lord and gave Him his undivided attention. The Bible records: *"Noah did everything exactly as God had commanded him"* (Genesis 6:22).

He built the ark to the Lord's precise specifications— and his family lived to enjoy the rainbow!

14

Esther didn't play it safe.

During the reign of the pagan King Xerxes, his wife was banished from the palace for disobedience. To search for a new queen, the king arranged a beauty pageant and chose a ravishing young woman named Esther to become his wife—unaware she was Jewish.

Through a series of events, the king ordered all Jews in the kingdom to be annihilated, yet Esther knew she was destined to save her people. Her commitment was so deeply embedded she said to herself, *"...if I perish, I perish"* (Esther 4:16 KJV).

What a selfless spirit! God saw this woman's heart and used Esther to deliver her people.

Shadrach, Meshach and Abednego didn't play it safe.

How would you like to be told to either worship a heathen idol or be tossed into a burning-hot furnace? That was the choice presented to the three Hebrew children who were ordered to bow before a golden image of King Nebuchadnezzar.

Armed only with a total trust in God, Shadrach, Meshach and Abednego laid their lives on the line, telling the king, *"If we are thrown into the blazing furnace, the God whom we serve is able to save us. He will rescue us from your power, Your Majesty. But even if he doesn't, Your Majesty can be sure that we will never serve your gods or worship the gold statue you have set up"* (Daniel 3:17-18).

The fire was intense, but these sold out Hebrews refused to bow—and by a miracle of God walked out of the flames unharmed. They weren't even singed!

Daniel didn't play it safe.

A sharp, intelligent Israelite named Daniel was captive in a foreign land when the king made a decree that any individual found praying to *anyone*—divine or human—for the next 30 days would be thrown into the lion's den.

This didn't phase Daniel at all! The minute he heard the decree had been signed, *"he went home and knelt down as usual in his upstairs room, with its windows open toward Jerusalem. He prayed three times a day, just as he had always done, giving thanks to his God"* (Daniel 6:10).

The government officials were watching and, angry at his blatant disobedience, threw Daniel right into the den of hungry lions. You can read what happened next in scripture; God shut the mouth of every lion and Daniel was set free!

Paul and Silas didn't play it safe.

In the city of Philippi, two evangelists for Christ, Paul and Silas delivered an evil spirit out of a slave woman who was a fortune teller. This didn't sit well with her owners, who hoped to make money from her "gift" of predicting the future. Protecting their financial interests, they had the two preachers thrown in prison.

Did that silence these preachers? Absolutely not! They were fully committed to praising the Lord. Now in jail, around midnight they started *"praying and singing hymns to God, and the other prisoners were listening"* (Acts 16:25).

The Lord was listening too. Suddenly there was such a violent earthquake the doors of that prison flew open and Paul and Silas were liberated!

All of these men and women shared one thing in common; they each had a fervent passion to serve God to the extent nothing else mattered—not even the threat of death. As Martin Luther King, Jr., said, "If a man hasn't discovered something he will die for, he isn't fit to live."

◆

"IF A MAN HASN'T DISCOVERED SOMETHING HE WILL DIE FOR, HE ISN'T FIT TO LIVE."

– MARTIN LUTHER KING, JR.

TOTAL LOVE!

You may wonder, "What is God truly looking for in me?"

All the Creator asks is for us to love Him—with every ounce of our being. His Word declares: *"...if you love the Lord your God with all your heart and soul, and if you worship him, then he will send the rains in their proper seasons...*[and you] *will have plenty to eat"* (Deuteronomy 11:13-14).

God loves you deeply, and what He desires is for you to reciprocate. I don't mean some hit-and-miss, half-hearted friendship that only works when it's convenient or when you find yourself in trouble. I'm talking about an "all out" love which demonstrates "absolutely nothing

—————◆————— or *no one* is more important."

THE LORD'S AFFECTION IS NEVER ONE SIDED.

Friend, we need to reach the place where we can truthfully tell the Lord, "Even if You never love me back, I will still love You!"

Fortunately, you don't need to worry about such a scenario. The Lord's affection is *never* one sided. God says, *"I love all who love me"* (Proverbs 8:17).

It's the Father's deep longing to find those who will love Him—so He can show Himself strong on their behalf. Even more, the Almighty wants to *prove* His abiding affection for us.

How does God demonstrate His unshakable love?

- **By giving His Son, Jesus Christ.** *"For God so loved the world, that he gave his only begotten Son, that whosoever believeth in Him should not perish, but have everlasting life"* (John 3:16 KJV).

- **By pouring out great blessings.** *"No good thing will the Lord withhold from those who*

18

do what is right" (Psalm 84:11). He has *"blessed us with every spiritual blessing... because we belong to Christ"* (Ephesians 1:3).

- **By giving us security.** As Paul exclaims: *"I am convinced that nothing can ever separate us from his love. Death can't, and life can't. The angels can't, and the demons can't. Our fears for today, our worries about tomorrow, and even the powers of hell can't keep God's love away"* (Romans 8:38).

From the dawn of creation to this very hour, the Lord has *never* stopped showing His compassion—and you can receive it today by simply opening you heart.

WHAT ABOUT YOUR FLAWS?

I smile when I hear a new Christian say, "I want to give the Lord my all, but I don't think I could ever live up to the high standards of men and women in Bible times."

Well, if you keep reading God's Word you'll quickly learn that people in the Old and New Testaments were not much different than we are today. Study the accounts of Moses, David or the apostle Peter and you'll meet men with major human flaws—including struggles with

19

compromise, inconsistency and lack of self-control.

Why did God use these "flawed" men for such awesome assignments? It was because the Almighty looked on the *inside* and recognized their deeply rooted love for Him.

When God chose Moses to lead His people out of Egypt, this "nobody" asked the Lord, *"But who am I to appear before Pharaoh?"* (Exodus 3:11). Yet, despite his insecurities, Moses became a mighty leader.

David's tryst with Bathsheba should have derailed his royal train. However, God saw something far greater. He found in David, *"a man after my own heart"* (Acts 13:22).

> **BEING FULLY COMMITTED MEANS TOTAL DEVOTION— SO RADICALLY IN LOVE WITH CHRIST THAT EVERYTHING ELSE FADES INTO OBSCURITY.**

Peter, one of Jesus' disciples, denied the Lord—not just once, but *three times*. Still, the Son of God reached beyond Peter's human frailties and totally restored him to ministry. Jesus asked, "Do You love me?"

Peter answered, "Lord, you know everything. You know I love You."

Jesus looked at him and said, *"Then feed my sheep"* (John 21:17).

Being fully committed means total devotion—so radically in love with Christ that everything else fades into obscurity.

TAKE OFF THE BRAKES!

Ask yourself this question: "What am I going to do with the rest of my life?"

Are you going to live "all out"—or play it safe?

Remember, *"The eyes of the Lord search the whole earth in order to strengthen those whose hearts are fully committed to him"* (2 Chronicles 16:9).

Sure, life has roads with hills and valleys, relationships which are broken and mended and reality that seems to fade in and out of focus. But what an adventure when, by faith, you take off the brakes of fear and give yourself totally to God's dream for your future.

Are you ready for the ride?

21

CHAPTER 2

THE YOU GOD IS SEARCHING FOR

I meet zealous, dedicated Christians who loudly—and sometimes *proudly*—tell the world, "I'm on a mission for the Lord!"

However, when you pin these people down, they can't articulate what they have specifically been called to do. They are just running around in circles, exhausting themselves with spiritual activity.

It's time to pause for a moment and realize that God is *also* on a mission. He is searching the earth for certain people to whom He can entrust distinct assignments.

The purpose for the search is not just a game of tag—where He touches you in a church service, then it's your turn to try and find Him again in a month or two when your favorite worship chorus is being sung.

God is serious! He's looking to find someone,

anyone—regardless of their status or age. He wants an individual He can rescue from aimlessly following the crowd, a person who will take on a heavenly task and be fully committed.

Our relationship with the Lord must be a *partnership*: you cannot do it without God, and God will not do it without you!

DO OR DIE!

I was 30 years old when the Lord unexpectedly interrupted my life. For the previous ten years I had been the associate pastor at one of the most influential churches in Fort Worth, Texas. Then God gave me a brand new assignment.

Hearing a voice from heaven as clear as anything I had ever experienced, Anna and I, with two small children, packed and moved to Grand Junction, Colorado.

There, in a run-down building with 19 people on our first Sunday, we birthed a new church with a mission of reaching the unreached. In the natural, the task looked daunting, if not impossible. For the first year we received no salary—living on the proceeds of selling our Texas home and Anna's car and support checks from our church back in Texas.

Talk about a "do or die" situation!

Opening my Bible, I read these words: *"See, I am doing a new thing!...do you not perceive it?"* (Isaiah 43:19 NIV).

Guess what! The Lord didn't fail us. Because we were fully committed, God's favor was evident—and eventually we were strongly supported. The Lord raised up a mighty church for His glory!

STEPPING INTO THE UNKNOWN

Are you ready to receive an assignment from heaven?

The person God is looking for doesn't need an impressive mile-long resume. They may not be the most talented or even the best educated. Instead, the man, woman or young person He will support is one who trusts Him completely—one with a "bet the farm" mentality!

ARE YOU WILLING TO FORFEIT YOUR SECURITY AND RELY ON GOD FOR YOUR TOMORROW?

Could you possibly be that person? Are you willing to forfeit your security and rely on God for your tomorrow?

In the words of an anonymous author, "When we come to the edge of all we know and are about to step off into the darkness of the unknown, of this we can be sure: either God will provide something solid for us to stand on, or He will teach us how to fly!"

Rest in the Father's promise: " *'For I know the plans I have for you,' declares the Lord, 'plans to prosper you and not to harm you, plans to give you hope and a future'"* (Jeremiah 12:11 NIV).

START BUILDING!

God not only implants a dream, He calls you to action. It's all well and good to harbor great ideas and lofty visions, but are you prepared to get your hands dirty—to dig the foundation and start building?

Pay close attention to the first three verses of the book of Psalms. *"Blessed is the man who does not walk in the counsel of the wicked or stand in the way of sinners or sit in the seat of mockers. But his delight is in the law of the Lord, and on his law he meditates day and night. He is like a tree planted by streams of water, which yields its fruit in season and whose leaf does not wither. Whatever he does prospers"* (Psalms 1:1-3 NIV).

> **UNLESS WE PICK UP OUR SHOVEL, WE ARE WASTING BOTH OUR TIME AND THE LORD'S.**

Re-read those last four words. It's not what he *thinks*, what he has *decided* or what he has been *exposed to*. It's what he *does!*

The person God seeks must be willing to build on what he has been given—moving into the construction mode. Unless we pick up our shovel, we are wasting both our time and the Lord's. *"For if any be a hearer of the word, and not a doer, he is like unto a man beholding his natural face in a glass"* (James 1:23 KJV).

Your pastor can teach, love, encourage and motivate you 24/7, yet if you choose to warm a chair rather than venture out in faith, God's purpose for you will be cut short.

Some mumble, "Well, I'm just waiting on God."

Instead, they need to open up their mind and understand God is patiently waiting for them!

WATER YOUR SEED

It's only natural to question what the Lord expects of you—and I believe God has already given the answer.

He has placed within each of us the seed of a dream. It may be latent, asleep, yet it's there. And the more time we spend in prayer and fellowship with Him, the more awakened and defined that vision becomes.

Remember this: what the Father places in your mind and heart is for you alone. Just as He has given you an unduplicated fingerprint, he stamps on your soul a unique assignment only you can fulfill.

What good is a God-given glimpse of your future if you fail to move forward and it withers like an unwatered vine.

MORE THAN A DREAM!

Joseph, the 17-year-old son of Jacob, was in a field with his brothers watching over a flock of sheep when he called his siblings to his side and announced: *"Listen to this dream...We were out in the field tying up bundles of grain. My bundle stood up, and then your bundles all gathered around and bowed low before it!"* (Genesis 37:6-7).

Can you imagine their displeasure? The nerve of their kid brother to even suggest such a thing! Their anger bubbled to the point these brothers threw Joseph in a pit—then sold him to a caravan of Ishmaelites headed for Egypt.

Now working in Pharaoh's palace, the dream God had implanted was never far from his mind. Even when he was unjustly sentenced to prison, this man from Judah used his gifts and talents to keep striving toward that objective, like a carpenter constructing a building.

This young man risked everything until the day arrived when he was elevated to governor of the land, placed in charge of the entire country.

Joseph's brothers—because of a famine in Israel—had no other option but to travel to Egypt and bow before the governor to plead for provisions to carry back to a hungry nation. Can you imagine their shock when they finally learned the person they knelt before was the brother they had so quickly disowned?

God placed Joseph in his unusual position to preserve Israel (Genesis 45:6-7). There was something far greater at work!

When the Lord gives a dream, it is for a divine purpose. That's why Joseph could say, *"As far as I am concerned, God turned into good what you meant for evil. He brought me to the high position I have today so I could save the lives of many people"* (Genesis 50:20).

HEART-DRIVEN ACTION

Far too many stand back and place all the responsibility on God—forgetting the Bible says, *"...faith without works is dead"* (James 2:20).

Without putting your hands to the plow there is no success or prosperity. It's belief *plus* action that brings abundance.

Let me tell you about a man named Hezekiah. During his day there were events happening in Judah that upset God—and there was great conflict in the land. It seemed the leaders were only concerned with their personal popularity.

At the young age of 25, Hezekiah stepped in to become King of Judah. Why did he triumph when others failed? It was a combination of heart-felt commitment and diligent work. The Bible records: *"In all that he did in the service of the Temple of God and in his efforts to follow the law and the commands, Hezekiah sought his God wholeheartedly. As a result, he was very successful"* (2 Chronicles 31:21).

> ◆
> **IT IS BELIEF PLUS ACTION THAT BRINGS ABUNDANCE.**

We see the same pattern surfacing when God placed a dream in the heart of Nehemiah to mend the broken walls of Jerusalem. Observe how scripture describes the progress: *"So we rebuilt the wall till all of it reached half its height, for the people worked with all their heart"* (Nehemiah 4:6 NIV).

What seemed like a hopeless project sprang into reality because of the desire God instilled *inside* them.

Could this gigantic undertaking have been completed without the Lord's help? Absolutely not, they would have grown weary and despondent. God *inspired* Nehemiah's workers until the job was finished.

THE DIVINE UNION!

To fulfill God's will, it takes a combined effort—you and the Almighty. Don't try to do it alone. Remember, *"Except the Lord build the house, they labor in vain that build it"* (Psalm 127:1).

———◆———

TO FULFILL GOD'S WILL, IT TAKES A COMBINED EFFORT—YOU AND THE ALMIGHTY.

This same principle is true whether you are laying stone or sharing the Gospel. The Bible tells us: *"And the disciples went everywhere and preached, and the Lord worked with them, confirming what they said by many miraculous signs"* (Mark 16:20).

It's a divine union! As David explained, *"Unless the Lord had been my help, my soul had almost dwelt in silence"* (Psalms 94:17). In other words, "Without God I'd be dead!"

EXECUTE THE PLAN

Imagine what the world would be like if we all lived to our full potential. God places a dream in our heart for a purpose—and if we don't build on that vision we have not only disappointed Him, we have squandered our future.

Let me share these three life-construction plans:

1. Build according to the pattern God gives you!

Don't waste your time and energy on a plan the Lord has inspired in your neighbor or a friend. Ask God what it is *you* must accomplish.

When the Lord called me to the city where I now pastor, He also revealed a pattern by which I was to build this particular church. I could not follow the blueprint He had given to Billy Graham or T.D. Jakes. I am not them!

The Lord showed me it was time to break out of my box-type thinking and follow the move of the Holy Spirit.

We need to come to the Lord with a clean slate for Him to write upon, saying, "Lord show me the steps I should take."

The Bible tells us, *"...when Moses was getting ready to build the Tabernacle, God gave him this warning: 'Be sure that you make everything according to the design I have shown you here on the mountain'"* (Hebrews 8:5).

It was God-given—specifically designed for Moses

31

and the children of Israel.

People still ask, "Pastor, tell me what I'm supposed to do!"

I wish I could, but that's between you and your Maker—and only revealed when you spend time in His presence.

———◆———
START BUILDING ACCORDING TO THE PATTERN INSTEAD OF THE PROBLEM.

Start building according to the pattern instead of the problem. Follow the voice that comes from above, not the chatter of those around you.

2. Do your homework and practice in private.

As children we all experienced faulty, hesitant steps, not to mention bumps and bruises. We didn't run until we learned to walk.

More than once my wife has walked into my office and found me preaching to the walls—or driving down the road talking to myself, rehearsing how I'm going to communicate a particular thought.

It's essential we do our homework and find the best information. King Solomon wrote: *"Commit yourself to instruction; attune your ears to hear words of knowledge"* (Proverbs 23:12). Then start sharpening your skills.

Young David didn't suddenly rise up and defeat the mighty Goliath. He had practice on the hills of Judea!

Here's what he told King Saul: *"I have been taking care of my father's sheep...When a lion or a bear comes to steal a lamb from the flock, I go after it with a club and take the lamb from its mouth. If the animal turns on me, I catch it by the jaw and club it to death. I have done this to both lions and bears, and I'll do it to this pagan Philistine, too, for he has defied the armies of the living God!"* (1 Samuel 17:34-37).

David rehearsed in private before his awesome public showdown.

3. Make the investment, then take the risk.

If you're looking for a place to build your portfolio, the greatest investment you'll ever make is in *yourself.*

THE GREATEST INVESTMENT YOU'LL EVER MAKE IS IN YOURSELF.

Equip your life through a career-skill seminar, a marriage retreat or a faith-building conference. Purchase some books, tapes or CD's that will broaden your horizons and open new avenues for growth.

Fortified with that knowledge, step out and take the kind of risk we've been discussing. Get out of the boat and start walking!

You worry, "What if I fail?"

You're not alone, God is right there, saying "Fear not!" Try one more time! Your life is not over at 32, 62 or 82. Keep building!

CAN YOU SEE IT?

Satan has painted a bull's eye target on your future. If he can damage what you envision by faith, he will destroy your progress.

- If you can't see yourself in a strong family, you'll never build one.
- Without visualizing yourself as a leader, it won't happen.
- If you never form a mental picture of achievement, you are destined for either mediocrity or failure.

◆

THE YOU GOD IS SEARCHING FOR IS A SOLD OUT, HEART-DRIVEN BELIEVER WHO IS PASSIONATE ABOUT SEEING THE LORD'S ONE-OF-A-KIND DREAM FULFILLED.

Of course, the enemy will always try to send someone to deflate your balloon and laugh at your dreams. That's why you must be careful with whom you share God's vision. But when you know the *source* of the criticism, you can tell Satan, "Get out of here! I'm not listening to your lies!"

YOUR INCREDIBLE FUTURE

The YOU God is searching for is a sold out, heart-driven believer who is passionate about seeing the Lord's one-of-a-kind dream fulfilled.

To quote the great evangelist, Dwight L. Moody, "The world has yet to see what God can do with a man fully consecrated to Him. By God's help, I aim to be that man."

Is that your prayer?

CHAPTER 3

TAKE CHARGE OF YOUR EMOTIONS

You are treading in dangerous territory when you allow your emotions to dictate your behavior.

Let me tell you about a Texan who took a hunting trip to Colorado. He and a local were walking along when they looked up and saw some ducks flying overhead. The Texan shot one of the ducks and it landed just across the fence—on someone else's property.

As he rushed to retrieve the bird, his hunting partner yelled, "Don't go over there. You've got to have permission from the owner before you cross his fence."

The Texan casually replied, "Nah, I don't need an okay. I'm an attorney from Dallas. I'll be all right."

Just as the man started to climb over the fence, the owner of the ranch spotted him, ran over and said, "Sir, around here if you shoot anything and it goes across the fence you have to ask permission to retrieve it. That's just the way it is!"

Indignant, the hunter snapped, "I don't think so, Scooter. I'm a Texas lawyer and we don't get permission for too many things." Then he added, "If I want to get the duck, I will. And if you don't like it, I'll just file a lawsuit against you and take you to court."

THE "THREE KICK RULE"

The rancher replied, "Now calm down. Here in Colorado we don't settle things in court. We just use what we call the 'three kick rule.'"

"What in the world is that?" asked the bewildered attorney.

"Well, it goes like this," the landowner began. "I'll just haul off and kick you as hard as I can three times, then you kick me back as hard as you can three times. And we will do this until somebody gives up—then the other person wins."

The Texan confidently smiled, "I think that will be just fine!"

The rancher said, "I'll go first," and he kicked the hunter in the shin with his steel-pointed boot. Wham! The Texan fell down in a heap. Next, the landowner proceeded to kick him hard two more times.

After rolling around on the ground in pain, the

attorney stood up—his legs and mouth were bleeding and one of his ribs felt cracked. Angry and dazed, he shouted, "Okay buddy, now it's my turn!"

The Colorado rancher retorted, "It's all right. I give up. You can have the duck!"

The Texan learned quite a lesson!

THINK FIRST!

We were all created as emotional beings, yet our "feelings" are neither good nor bad. They can be helpful or harmful, depending on how we choose to use them.

The truth is: God never told you how you should *feel* about anything—not even about Him. Instead, He teaches you how to *think*, and consequently, the right emotions will follow.

> ◆
> **GOD NEVER TOLD YOU HOW YOU SHOULD FEEL ABOUT ANYTHING —NOT EVEN HIM.**

Feelings are directly linked to your thoughts. For example, just because you *feel* discouraged does not mean you must remain that way. Changing your thoughts can cause your darkest fears to literally disappear, but it takes self-discipline to control what takes place in the mind-emotion-behavior cycle.

LOOK OUT FOR THAT SERPENT!

There's a *reason* we are admonished to "fix our

thoughts" on what is true, honorable, pure, lovely, admirable, excellent and worthy of praise (Philippians 4:8). Why? Because doing this changes our entire outlook and lifts us to higher ground.

Negative thoughts are poison to our emotions. They are like a virus which, if left unchecked, can weaken and ultimately destroy our entire system.

Why beat yourself up, put yourself down or throw yourself into a guilt drip over a sin you have already confessed to the Father—something He has forgiven and forgotten?

The moment such thoughts surface, recognize they are not from God and dismiss them.

> —— ◆ ——
> **NEGATIVE THOUGHTS ARE POISON TO OUR EMOTIONS.**

If you were to go home tonight and find a rattlesnake curled up in the middle of your living room floor, how would you react? Would you calmly say, "Well, I'll get to that later. There's something I want to watch on television." Or, "I'm a little hungry. I think I'll get a bite to eat."

No! You'd either call 911 or find a shotgun! You would do whatever was necessary to remove that reptile from your house. Why? Because it is extremely dangerous.

Do you realize wrong thoughts are just as harmful? When they rear their ugly head, do not procrastinate and say, "I'll take care of them later." If you refuse to take immediate action, those thoughts can be disastrous.

When your mind paints a negative scenario, don't accept it or say, "Oh, this is really going to be bad!" If this is your reaction, you may wind up like Job, who said, *"What I always feared has happened to me. What I dreaded has come to be"* (Job 3:25).

WHAT'S ON YOUR MIND?

Become totally aware of what is happening in you thought process. The instant you feel anger, resentment or *any* negative emotions begin to rise, stop and reflect:

- "I'm feeling sad. What am I thinking about right now?
- "I'm feeling worried. What is on my mind?"
- "I'm feeling defeated. What thoughts are triggering this emotion?"

Self-control involves exercising restraint—and it begins by taking charge of your mind and body (what the Bible calls "flesh").

Here's how the apostle Paul explains it: *"...those who are still under the control of their sinful nature can never please God. But you are not controlled by your sinful nature* [the flesh]. *You are controlled by the Spirit if you*

41

have the Spirit of God living in you. (And remember that those who do not have the Spirit of Christ living in them are not Christians at all)" (Romans 8:8-9).

Next, Paul gives us one of the most powerful statements you will ever read. He declares, *"So, dear brothers and sisters, you have no obligation whatsoever to do what your sinful nature urges you to do"* (v.12).

The decision is *yours,* not God's since you are the gate keeper of your emotions—with the ability to let them in or lock them out.

DON'T TAKE THE EASY WAY OUT

Our *flesh* constantly tries to pull us in the wrong direction. It causes us to say the wrong words, watch the wrong things and react in the wrong way. Consequently, by yielding to our sinful nature we become miserable failures, and even worse. *"For if you keep on following it, you will perish"* (v.13).

Thank God, there is a better choice: *"But if through the power of the Holy Spirit you turn from it and its evil deeds, you will live. For all who are led by the Spirit of God are children of God"* (vv.13-14).

It gets even better! Paul tells us not to be as cowering and fearful slaves, rather we should behave as *"God's very own children, adopted into His family— calling 'Father, dear Father'"* (v.15).

And since we are His children, *"we will share in his treasures—for everything God gives to his Son, Christ, is ours, too. But if we are to share his glory, we must also share his suffering"* (v.17).

When we are strong and resist the tug of the flesh it often *feels* like suffering, but God's Word tells us that's exactly what we must do.

It is always easier to say what you *feel* like saying, eat what you *feel* like eating, and sit in front of a television set instead of getting some exercise.

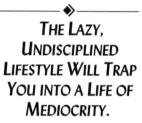

THE LAZY, UNDISCIPLINED LIFESTYLE WILL TRAP YOU INTO A LIFE OF MEDIOCRITY.

But the lazy, undisciplined lifestyle will trap you into a life of mediocrity.

WHEN ARE WE AT RISK?

There are certain times when we are especially vulnerable regarding yielding to our emotions—to allow our feelings to rule the day and determine our behavior. Those moments include:

1. When we are hurt by words or deeds.

We pout, "Did you hear what he said about me?" Or, "Why did she need to act like that?"

In such moments, our thinking often becomes clouded and we try to compensate in unexpected ways.

Sadly, when emotions cry out, "Make me feel better,"

many look for comfort or escape in alcohol, sexual affairs or pornography. They want a quick "feel good" hit, yet their search ultimately leaves them hollow.

Please do not allow feelings to take over your decision making—"Well, I'm mad. I think I'll do this!"

Resist Satan's bait. Instead, make choices *only* by the leading of the Holy Spirit.

2. When we are weary.

God knew what He was doing when He told us, "Labor six days and rest on the seventh."

How can we be expected to make wise choices when our minds are numb and our bodies are exhausted from overwork? We need a break!

I've encountered my share of intelligent people who made foolish decisions—not because they were bad people, simply because they were tired.

If you find yourself in such a predicament, don't be hasty. Say, "Let me think about that for a while."

Get alone with God and recharge your tired body. Remember, *"He gives strength to the weary and increases the power of the weak"* (Isaiah 40:29 NIV).

3. When we aren't guarding our thinking.

A man confided in his pastor, "I'm trying to live a positive life, but my emotions are getting the best of me."

"Tell me about it," said the minister.

"Well, my wife left, my business partner took advantage of me. It's all I think about—what they said and how they broke my heart. As a result I go around feeling despondent and can't seem to get a handle on my feelings."

The pastor responded, "Sir, you don't have an emotional problem; your emotions are acting just as God created them to. If you meditate on sad thoughts, you will encourage sad feelings. When you start dwelling on what the Lord promises, positive feelings will follow."

He reassured the man, "You don't have an emotional problem, you have a *thinking* problem."

Why wait for some perfect moment to experience joy? Follow the example of the apostle Paul, who said, *"I think myself happy"* (Acts 36:1 KJV).

> ◆
>
> **"YOU DON'T HAVE AN EMOTIONAL PROBLEM, YOU HAVE A THINKING PROBLEM."**

DECLARE IT!

When negative thoughts filter into your mind, take these two steps: (1) Reject them immediately. (2) Replace such thoughts with God's unchanging Word.

Today—and *every* day— declare:

- "This is the day the Lord has made. I will rejoice and be glad in it."

- "God is able to do exceedingly abundantly beyond what I ask or think."
- "I am an heir of God through Christ."
- "If God be for me, who can be against me?"
- "Nothing shall separate me from the love of Christ."
- "All things work together for good to those who love God and are called according to His purpose."

IT'S TIME TO BE AGGRESSIVE!

If your mind is not filled with God's blessings, there will be a vacuum—and Satan is only too eager to rush in and fill the void.

When you are sick and start thinking, "I'm never going to get well," replace it with, "Lord, you said, 'By your stripes we are healed!'"

If you worry, "I am never going to meet my goals in life," say, "Lord, you declared that if I put you first, You would crown my efforts with success."

> BE BOLD AND AGGRESSIVE, KNOWING SATAN CANNOT TELL THE TRUTH.

When your innermost thoughts cause you to feel lonely and unhappy, tell God, "You told me that if I delight in You, You would give me the desire of my heart."

Be bold and aggressive, knowing Satan cannot tell the truth.

Jesus didn't mince words when the religious leaders of His day announced, "We are the children of Abraham."

The Lord looked these hypocrites straight in the eye and told them: *"If God were your Father, you would love me, because I have come to you from God. I am not here on my own, but he sent me. Why can't you understand what I am saying? It is because you are unable to do so! For you are the children of your father the Devil, and you love to do the evil things he does. He was a murderer from the beginning and has always hated the truth. There is no truth in him. When he lies, it is consistent with his character; for he is a liar and the father of lies. So when I tell the truth, you just naturally don't believe me!"* (John 8:42-45).

SATAN'S LIES VS. GOD'S TRUTH

Try a new offensive against the devil. When he crowds your thoughts with fear, turn it around on him. Since it's impossible for the devil to be honest, you can rest assured the direct *opposite* of Satan's pronouncement is what's

SINCE IT'S IMPOSSIBLE FOR THE DEVIL TO BE HONEST, YOU CAN REST ASSURED THE DIRECT OPPOSITE OF SATAN'S PRONOUNCEMENT IS WHAT'S ABOUT TO TAKE PLACE.

about to take place.

If he whispers, "Your family will never be saved," reply, "Well, thank you, Father of Lies, that means God's Word is true. He said He would save me—and my household!"

When Satan tells you, "You're career is about to crumble," exclaim, "Thank you for the confirmation. God is opening the windows of heaven and rebuking the devourer for my sake!"

His lies are a great indicator of what the Lord desires to pour into your life.

I remember when we purchased the land for our new church, we were told by an attorney at a public planning board meeting in our city, "You folks bought the wrong property. There's no way you'll be able to build a church on that corner."

---◆---

JUST BECAUSE YOU'VE DECIDED TO GO FULL SPEED AHEAD DOESN'T MEAN YOU NEED TO BE RIDING AN EMOTIONAL ROLLER COASTER.

After the rather heated session, I drove home thinking, "Thank you, Mr. Enemy. You have just confirmed the fact we are going to build a worship center on that very property. We believe what God said, not you."

Today, the church stands triumphantly on that land.

THINK "HEAD FIRST!"

Just because you've decided to go full speed ahead

doesn't mean you need to be riding an emotional roller coaster. Not at all. Ask the Lord to take control of your thoughts and everything else will fall in line with His will.

Take the advice of the apostle Paul who says, *"You need to use your head and test your feelings"* (Philippians 1:9 (TM).

Make a commitment to think before acting, to believe before behaving. What a fantastic difference it will make!

CHAPTER 4

FULLY COMMITTED TO MY WIFE –BUT STILL A JERK SOMETIMES!

Out of curiosity I looked up the definition of the word *commitment* and it read: "to obligate or bind; the state of being emotionally or intellectually loyal to an ideal or course of action. To promise, pledge or vow, to be obligated to another."

Wow! I'm glad it didn't say "to be perfect" or I would have been in deep trouble!

I know how to be loyal and I understand what it means to keep something or someone as a top priority, but I certainly don't pass the "perfection test."

Anna and I met in high school and were first best friends. We fell in love, married, became parents and are now proud grandparents. However, it was only after 27 years of marriage that I learned how to load the dishwasher!

WHAT'S YOUR PRIORITY?

Being fully committed to your spouse doesn't mean you will only hit home runs and have no strike-outs or errors. Nor does it guarantee you won't get on the other person's nerves. If that was the criteria my wife was looking for, I've blown it more times than I can count. And if perfection was God's measuring stick, we would all sadly fail.

Total commitment means just that—always having the other person as your number one priority for love, longing and loyalty.

CELEBRATE YOUR DIFFERENCES

As a pastor, I have enjoyed the wonderful privilege of uniting several hundred couples in marriage. In the process, there have been rare occasions when I looked at a young man and woman and thought, "They are such a perfect match."

However, most of the time I see polar opposites—people who are as different from each other as cats and dogs. I can't help but think their desire to spend the rest of their lives together must reflect God's sense of humor!

In reality, two contrasting personalities will each bring something of value into the life of the other—which results in growth and personal development.

I am convinced the goal in marriage should be that two people who come together can do far more for God than they could ever accomplish as individuals.

In almost every case, it's the *differences* which give the union it's strength. But it is also these same distinctions which demand an extraordinary commitment to the relationship so it can weather life's ups and downs—and morph the marriage into something truly amazing.

———— ❖ ————

I AM CONVINCED THE GOAL IN MARRIAGE SHOULD BE THAT TWO PEOPLE WHO COME TOGETHER CAN DO FAR MORE FOR GOD THAN THEY COULD EVER ACCOMPLISH AS INDIVIDUALS.

GOD'S WEATHER FORECAST

It's inevitable! Strong winds will blow—against couples who know the Lord and those who don't. We *all* face difficulties.

Just after Jesus finished teaching His first public message on "How to have a Blessed Life"—the Beatitudes—He gives us a story concerning building a home life which will go the distance.

Jesus said those who listen to His teaching and obey Him are wise, *"like a person who builds a house on solid rock. Though the rain comes in torrents and the floodwaters rise and the winds beat against that house, it won't collapse, because it is built on rock. But anyone who hears my teaching and ignores it is foolish, like a person who builds a house on sand. When the rains and floods come and the winds beat against that house, it will fall with a mighty crash"* (Matthew 7:24-27).

From this we learn none of us are sheltered from the storms—even those who know Christ. The difference, however, is the capacity for endurance—the ability to survive the deluge with little or no lasting damage.

GET READY!

There are two particular disturbances all married couples will face:

1. Financial storms

These have little to do with the amount of money you earn; they usually concern the mutual agreement of how the funds are spent.

2. Communication storms

———◆———
AN EXCHANGE OF WORDS DOES NOT GUARANTEE UNDERSTANDING IS TAKING PLACE.

Men and woman express themselves differently and each need to learn (then re-learn) how to share their feelings.

Many couples believe communication simply means "more talking." While this may be important, an exchange of words does not guarantee understanding is taking place.

"YOU MIGHT BE A MAN"

In my 20-plus years as a counselor, with a Master's

degree in Marriage and Family Counseling, I've come to appreciate the necessity of adding as much humor and "lightness" as possible into what can often become quite heated conflicts on the topic of marriage.

I try to let women know that men are really not too complicated. In the style of Jeff Foxworthy:

> — "If you want to kill what you eat…you might be a man.
> — If you've only had one hairstyle for your entire life…you might be a man.
> — If you can go to the bathroom without a support group…you might be a man.
> — If you can go over to a buddies house without having to bring a little gift…you might be a man."

Do any of these hit close to home?

WHO'S TALKING?

Marriage counselor and author Gary Smalley reports that on any given day a man will speak 20,000 words while a woman will utter 30,000. So, when a husband arrives home, he's probably already used up his daily quota, but his wife still has 10,000 left over for the remainder of the evening!

My wife says the reason women use so many more words is because they need to repeat everything at least twice to their husbands. She is probably onto something!

However, the most critical area where communication

is absolutely vital is the topic of our *needs*. Husbands and wives must be able to share their personal desires with their mate—especially regarding satisfaction and security.

REAL PEOPLE, REAL NEEDS

In Dr. Willard Harley's book, *His Needs, Her Needs*, he gives us the five top basic requirements of a woman and a separate list for a man. These needs must be communicated, understood and committed to by every married couple.

Her Needs:	**His Needs:**
1. Affection	1. Sexual fulfillment
2. Conversation	2. Recreational
3. Honesty and	companionship
openness	3. An attractive spouse
5 . Financial support	4. Domestic support
5. Family commitment	5. Admiration

I highly recommend Dr. Harley's book to couples for the purpose of breaking "catch 22's" while trying to share basic needs with your mate.

GET IT RIGHT!

It's impossible to count the number of times I've counseled a husband and wife in my office and, in order to make any progress in our discussion, I have had to ask the man, "Tell your wife what you want to say."

Then I have her repeat to me what she "thought" she heard him say—until she gets it right. Next, I repeat the process with the wife speaking, and the husband repeating what he thought he heard her say.

In some instances it takes 15 minutes to clarify two or three simple sentences. Only then do the interpersonal problems begin to see the light of day.

This process is biblical: *"Reliable communication permits progress"* (Proverbs 13:17 TLB).

WHAT ABOUT THE DETAILS?

Healthy interaction requires two ingredients:

1. Say enough stuff!
2. Say the right stuff!

I analyzed my own daily routine and realized that at work I communicate in *megabytes*, yet at home I only use short *sound bites*. At the end of a 12-hour day my wife can ask, "How did things go today?"

Well, I can usually wrap it up in about two minutes because men have a knack of leaving out the details.

I didn't realize I was doing this until my grown daughter called our house one evening and asked to speak with her mother. She said, "I have something really funny to tell her about your grandkids—and you can get the story

"I HAVE SOMETHING REALLY FUNNY TO TELL HER ABOUT YOUR GRANDKIDS —AND YOU CAN GET THE STORY FROM MOM."

from Mom."

I asked, "Why can't you just tell me and let me relate it to her?"

I was surprised by her answer. She said, "Dad, you will forget and leave out too many good details when repeating the story. I'll just tell her and she will fill you in."

To be honest, I was slightly insulted, yet she was absolutely right!

SPEAK LIFE!

In order for there to be good dialog there has to be *enough* of it—and the right kind. Scripture tells us: *"Let no corrupt communication proceed out of your mouth, but only that which is good and edifying, that it may*

———— ◆ ————
IN ORDER FOR
THERE TO BE GOOD
DIALOG THERE HAS
TO BE ENOUGH OF
IT—AND THE
RIGHT KIND.

minister grace to the hearers" (Ephesians 4:29 KJV). W h a t powerful advice. The word *edify* means to build up, or to enrich. And *grace* is unearned or unmerited favor.

These are the key ingredients we must apply to *all* our relationships—not only with our spouse, but with our family, friends, and even *strangers*.

Without question, there is always something negative we can say about another person, yet when we do, look out!

Words have creative power and cause things to exist. That's why you must learn to speak *life* into your mate—even when the kind words you are verbalizing may not have been earned that particular day.

We need to constantly encourage one another.

LIGHTEN UP!

Far too many marriages suffer from what I call "a terminal case of seriousness." They've lost the childlike qualities which add excitement and joy to everyday events.

I'm sure you have observed how children have the innate ability to think *everything* is funny.

When most couples look back on their days of dating, one of the major attractions which drew them to their eventual life partner was usually that person's ability to make them laugh.

I married a woman who loves to have fun and we pastor a church filled with people who know how to smile. It's a healthy condition and a wonderful combination since the Bible tells us, *"A cheerful heart is good medicine"* (Proverbs 17:22).

> **IF YOUR BROW IS WRINKLED AND YOU ARE SINKING INTO SOMBER THOUGHTS, ASK THE LORD FOR HELP.**

If your brow is wrinkled and you are sinking into somber thoughts, ask the Lord for help. *"He will...fill your mouth with laughter and your lips with shouts of joy"* (Job 8:21).

I was recently speaking at a men's breakfast in another city on the subject, "Marriage and Family Life." Shortly after being introduced I told the distinguished group, "I have been married for 28 years." As they broke into applause I quickly added, "to seven different women!"

You should have seen these men scramble to stifle their congratulations! Of course, I was only joking, but it relaxed the tone and set the stage for an enjoyable session.

WHAT MAKES A MARRIAGE LAST?

My wife's parents were married 54 years before her father went to be with the Lord—and my parents celebrated 52 years prior to my dad making the same journey.

What was the secret of these long-lasting relationships? It wasn't the fact they each found Miss Right and Mr. Right. Such people do not exist. Instead, they discovered Miss Almost and Mr. Close Enough—and made the commitment to work together on smoothing the rough edges.

> ❖
>
> **MATRIMONY DOESN'T LAST 30, 40 OR 50 YEARS WITHOUT TOTAL DEDICATION ON THE PART OF EACH PARTNER.**

Matrimony doesn't last 30, 40 or 50 years without total dedication on the part of each partner. We are fallible—and yes, we sin.

When two imperfect people come together their strength and longevity is not found in their perfection, rather it lies in their love and commitment to God and each other.

IT'S ALL OR NOTHING!

A few days after the horrific 9/11 attack by terrorists on the World Trade Center in New York, I found myself thinking again and again about the innocent people who were trapped inside those towers. I envisioned the panic, the confusion, the ultimate reality—and their frantic attempts to escape.

My heart was deeply touched as I read the accounts of those who helped others get out of the blazing inferno.

> **I ENVISIONED THE PANIC, THE CONFUSION, THE ULTIMATE REALITY—AND THEIR FRANTIC ATTEMPTS TO ESCAPE.**

I imagined what it would have been like if Anna and I were in one of those towers when, unexpectedly, a 747 crashed through the windows. How would we have reacted when smoke filled the building and we felt the flames of hell itself?

Without question, we would have been stunned and overcome with fear. However, of one thing I have no doubt: we would have both made it out of the building together—or we wouldn't have made it at all!

When total commitment is the priority of two people, it's all or nothing.

THE POWER OF A VOW

After years of being a marriage and family counselor, you would think as a husband I would always get things right—wrong! The truth is, I make my fair share of blunders.

61

What I can *always* offer is to be a committed, faithful husband. And since it is mutual, there's not a doubt we will endure any setbacks and weather any hardships together.

This is the same vow I made to the Lord.

I was only twelve years old when I accepted Jesus as my personal Savior. Then I "super-sized" that relationship at 16 when I accepted His call on my life for ministry.

Have I been a perfect child of God? Not quite—and He knows it. In the words of David *"As a father has compassion on his children, so the Lord has compassion on those who fear him; for he knows how we are formed, he remembers that we are dust."* (Psalm 103:13 NIV).

Instead of chastising me for my shortcomings, the Lord, in His mercy, loves me!

---◆---

IT IS ONLY THROUGH THE COVENANT RELATIONSHIP I HAVE WITH HIM THAT I UNDERSTAND HOW TO BE FULLY COMMITTED TO MY WIFE AND FAMILY.

YOUR COVENANT RELATIONSHIP

Remember, *"Therefore, there is now no condemnation for those who are in Christ Jesus, because through Christ Jesus the law of the Spirit of life set me free from the law of sin and death"* (Romans 8:1-2 NIV).

The Lord has first place in my life—and always will. It is only through the covenant I have with Him that I understand how to be fully committed to my wife and family.

Friend, on a scale of one to ten, your faults and failures rate as a "zero" when compared with your love and loyalty to your family and to the Lord.

Be a vow-keeper. Stay committed!

Chapter 5

Rock-Solid!

Tony Chain was 37 years old and G. R. Hershel was 39. They had been hunting partners and best friends for the past 15 seasons.

On September 1, 1989, the opening day of duck season in Alaska, they beached their boat at an area known as Duck Flats and began to walk through the marshy land where they would begin hunting.

As Tony walked forward, he suddenly began to sink—first to his knees and then to his waist. It seemed like only seconds until his left wader became filled with mud and he frantically cried out, "Quicksand! Help!"

G.R. rushed over to help, but suddenly knew that he, too, was about to be trapped. So, reluctantly, he left Tony in a desperate attempt to find help.

Both men knew the area well. And with that knowledge came an understanding of the unpredictable tides that could sweep through the exact spot where Tony was trapped—rising as much as one foot every 12 minutes.

ONE LAST ATTEMPT

Slowly sinking, Tony finally heard the welcoming hum of a helicopter in the distance. G. R. had managed to call for assistance from a nearby air base. The chopper landed as close as possible and rescue personnel were rushing toward the trapped hunter.

As the team tried to reach Tony—who was now up to his neck—they too became stuck and were unable to help even themselves! That's when the waters began to quickly rise leaving time for only one last rescue attempt.

The pilot maneuvered the helicopter directly over Tony and the trapped men, lowered the lines, carefully hoisted them from the mud, and was able to set them down on firm, solid ground.

"IT SEEMED LIKE HOURS BEFORE HELP ARRIVED."

These men were airlifted from the quicksand at 1:45 P.M.—and just fifteen minutes later water totally covered the area where they had been.

Tony said later, "It seemed hours before help arrived. I thought about my wife who had died one year earlier of cancer at the age of 32—and of our three children and how they would make it without a Father. I worried about the tides and how long I had left."

Thank God, Tony lived to tell of his adventure.

Out of the Pit

We read of a similar experience in Psalm 40. This time, however, it's not the story of a couple of hunters in Alaska. It's about David, the lowly shepherd boy who became a king.

> *"I waited patiently for the Lord to help me,*
> *and he turned to me and heard my cry.*
> *He lifted me out of the pit of despair,*
> *out of the mud and the mire.*
> *He set my feet on solid ground and steadied me*
> *as I walked along.*
> *He has given me a new song to sing,*
> *a hymn of praise to our God.*
> *Many will see what he has done and be*
> *astounded.*
> *They will put their trust in the Lord."*
> —Psalm 40:1-3

Time for Testing

You don't have to look far these days to find someone whose life is in turmoil. I know most Christians believe God could rescue them out of a difficult situation, but do they believe—*really* believe—He could deliver them from an *impossible* situation?

In Matthew 7, Jesus contrasts the difference between the person who anchors his life to God's principles and one who doesn't.

The individual who ignores the life-laws of the Almighty is compared to the man who builds his house upon sand—unsteady ground that won't provide a sturdy reliable foundation when the winds start howling.

However, the person who *does* heed and obey the Lord's command is described as a man who builds his life on a solid rock. And, regardless of the storm it will stand.

BOMBINGS! MURDERS!

Without a doubt, we are living through what can only be described as "perilous times" with *"Men's hearts failing them for fear"* (Luke 21:26 KJV).

There was a time when Americans felt far more safe and secure in their homeland than in recent months.

Gone are the days when we displayed an untouchable attitude. We turned on the news and saw suicide bombings in Israel, political murders in Chechnya and our embassies being blown up in the Middle East and Africa.

We may have empathized with these people, but deep down felt, "This will never happen here! We live in the most powerful and protected nation in the world!"

Now we awaken to daily headlines of *Economic Crisis! Terror! War!*

A September morning in Manhattan changed

everything. Now we walk into airports to see armed guards and pass through ultra-tight security.

STARTING OVER

People once felt a strong sense of stability in their financial savings program. They worked hard and had a plan mapped out for their future—and watched their portfolio grow.

I talked with one friend who, after 30-plus years of saving for retirement saw his nest-egg dwindle away because of market fluctuations. He shook his head, saying, "I don't know if I can ever recover those funds."

THE CORPORATE BLOODBATH IN OUR NATION HAS TAKEN ITS TOLL.

Workers who once said, "At least I have my job," are also nervous. The corporate bloodbath in our nation has taken its toll. Hard working, experienced people who have been with a company for 15, 20 or even 25 years have been given pink slips without warning—needing to start over in their late 40s or 50s. For many, job security is a fading memory.

One area we have always considered unshakable is that of family life—the people God surrounds us with.

Yet, not a week goes by when I don't hear of relationships which have been drastically changed due to bad decisions. An ungodly media has torn at the fabric of marriage, sexual orientation, faith and values.

FIVE PROMISES

There is an old hymn of the church I still love to sing: "On Christ the Solid Rock I stand, all other ground is sinking sand."

What is the "other ground" so unstable and uncertain? It is our career, our health, our family and our nation.

There's only one Rock we can depend on. And an "all out" relationship with Him is our only source of true permanence and stability. *"The Lord lives! Praise be to my Rock! Exalted be God, the Rock, my Savior!"* (2 Samuel 47 NIV).

When you choose to stand on the firm foundation of Christ, here are five promises you can always count on:

1. A Rock-solid love.

Next to food and water, the most basic need of man is to be loved. We all long to be accepted and cherished as the person God made us to be.

Babies can die without enough affection and the lives of teenagers have been derailed by the lack of it.

From experience I can tell you that when you have a personal connection to the Lord you'll understand what it means to be held safe and secure in His everlasting arms. As the psalmist writes: *"Surely your goodness and unfailing love will pursue me all the days of my life"* (Psalm 23:6).

2. A Rock-solid pardon from past sin.

No one forgives us like Jesus. When we make mistakes—and we will—our Savior longs to pardon and bring us back to a closer walk with Him.

Not only will He forgive, but He will completely forget the incident. Can you think of anyone else who has that ability? I certainly can't. Some people will remember your faults longer than even you!

> SOME PEOPLE WILL REMEMBER YOUR FAULTS LONGER THAN EVEN YOU!

I love the story of the woman who went to a department store and found a blouse she wanted to purchase. She took it to the cashier and asked, "What does this tag mean? It says 'Shrink Resistant'"?

The surprised clerk replied, "Well, it will shrink, but it really doesn't want to!"

Something similar happens when we truly understand God's complete pardon. It's not that we don't can't sin, but we lose our motivation toward iniquity. We don't *want to* anymore!

3. A Rock-solid power.

You can find a strength beyond yourself:

- A power to love instead of hate.
- A power to control your impulses and change bad habits.

71

■ A power to forgive when you have been wronged.

This hidden stamina raises your esteem and self-worth. It allows you to walk into a room filled with confidence instead of arrogance.

You will look at life's impossibilities as challenges you can and *will* conquer. It is the same mighty power that caused a boy with only a slingshot to slay a giant!

God was watching David, and promised: *"Your family and your kingdom are permanently secured. I'm keeping my eye on them! And your royal throne will always be there, rock solid"* (2 Samuel 7:16 TM).

———◆———

HE WILL TURN YOUR WORK INTO A KINGDOM-BUILDING ADVENTURE WITH HIM.

4. A Rock-solid purpose and direction.

God will begin to unfold for you a course of action that involves more than a daily grind. He will turn your work into a Kingdom-building adventure with Him. The Lord will encourage you to take risks, step up to new challenges and go for it!

King Solomon tells us to seek *"knowledge, and wisdom for your soul—Get that and your future's secured, your hope is on solid rock"* (Proverbs 24:14 TM).

5. A Rock-solid assurance of knowing where you are going when you die.

It's difficult to explain, but when you have a total assurance of where you're headed after you pass from this earth, the less the world feels like home. We have the marvelous promise of something that will last forever.

When my father died I will never forget the peace he had, knowing he was going home to be with his Lord. There was no fear, but a calm, blessed assurance that "something better was coming."

This undaunted faith allowed him to face pain and loss with total peace.

COLLECTING CASH!

When I was about 10 years old, my sister—who was a college freshman—played "Monopoly" with me whenever she came home on a class break.

I loved the play money and my goal was to hang onto it as long as I could. My objective was to quickly pass GO and collect $200.00 more for my stockpile.

She, however, would spend her paper cash to buy utilities or property, then put hotels on them.

Of course, when I rolled the dice to try to hurry around the playing board, I would inevitably land on a space she owned and would have to give her rent. It didn't take long for her to win, and after each victory, with a little smirk on her face, she would say, "One of these days day you'll learn how to play this game."

"PAY UP!"

That day came sooner than she thought! Every Saturday I practiced with anyone who would take the time to play the game with me. Then, on my sister's next holiday break, I was ready and waiting!

This time I bought everything I could—adding houses and hotels on every property possible. I was ecstatic when my business-major big sister couldn't move without landing on spaces I owned. "Pay up!" I giddily exclaimed

It wasn't long before she was completely bankrupt. I had won!

Just as I was about to spend a little more time rubbing it in, my sister had one more lesson to teach me. She said, "That's great, but now it all goes back in the box."

Well, I didn't want to put it away. I begged to leave it in plain view so I could brag to everyone. If I could, I would have had the whole board bronzed—just as it was!

But she was right. It would all go back in the box to be played by someone else another day.

IT'S ALL GOING BACK!

Have you ever thought of the fact that everything in life goes back in a box—so to speak? Nothing on this earth is going to last forever. Your job, your bank accounts, your accomplishments, your family, your health—and one day even your body goes into a box. The only thing that won't be left behind is your soul.

Many learn the rules of the *acquiring* game and play it well, not realizing the time will come when it's all going to disappear.

Why not give yourself fully to the only thing that will last forever—a sold out, on fire, all out life which will lead to an eternity with Christ. *"Trust in the Lord always, for the Lord God is the eternal Rock"* (Isaiah 26:4).

All other ground is sinking sand!

CHAPTER 6

DID YOU HEAR THE MOUTH ON THAT GUY?

It's amazing what skilled surgeons can accomplish by repairing a burned or scarred body through skin grafting. What was once unsightly, suddenly becomes beautiful.

Arborists, "tree surgeons" accomplish something quite similar by grafting one tree to another—giving the new plant the ability to tolerate certain adverse soil conditions and thrive.

Did you know God also has a grafting process? James talks about it when he writes: *"Wherefore lay apart all filthiness and superfluity of naughtiness, and receive with meekness the engrafted word, which is able to save your souls"* (James 1:21 KJV).

The word *graft* means "to stick."

You can hear a million words preached from the pulpit—and even read the Bible from cover to cover a dozen times. Yet, God's Word does not benefit you until you allow it to *stick* to your soul. And the ultimate proof the Word has become active is when it starts pouring out of your own mouth.

DON'T SABOTAGE YOUR PROGRESS

In this book we've talked about making changes in your marriage, career and finances, but they are not going to happen overnight. It's a process. And when you take the steps we've been discussing you are well on your way to receiving God's blessings.

However, you will sabotage your progress if the words you utter don't reflect the transformation you have gone through. What you speak *seals* what you have received.

To insure you won't drift back into your old lifestyle, make certain your mouth parallels where you are headed.

"WHAT'S HAPPENED?"

Since scripture has the power to radically change your life, I believe your friends are going to notice the difference. In fact, some of those you hang around with might become annoyed or frustrated because your thinking and speaking is so new. They no longer hear you say, "I can't stand my boss!" or "Married life is the

78

pits!" The curse words that once peppered your conversation have disappeared.

Now you are enthused with living—"I'm excited about my job," and "My wife and I have never been happier!"

They look at you as if you've lost your mind, and ask, "What's happened? You've never talked this way before!"

A NEW LEVEL

Your words have incredible power—they can give life or become a weapon that wounds, even kills.

For example, two young adults can date for months or years and enjoy a thousand conversations. Yet, in a moment when you least expect it, out slips those three little words, "I love you!"

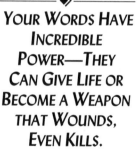

YOUR WORDS HAVE INCREDIBLE POWER—THEY CAN GIVE LIFE OR BECOME A WEAPON THAT WOUNDS, EVEN KILLS.

Suddenly, everything changes. You have now magnified the reality of the relationship and taken it to a whole new level.

The same thing is true with anger. You think, "I can't stand this person any longer," yet the moment you vent those feelings and yell, "I hate you!" something in that relationship dies.

God's Word speaks to this issue when it says: *"Death*

and life are in the power of the tongue" (Proverbs 18:21 KJV).

ONLY ONE DIRECTION!

I'm sure you've heard the phrase, "He speaks with a forked tongue," or "She talks out of both sides of her mouth!"

It's beyond me how some people can say:

- "I'm believing God for victory, but I don't really see how I'm going to get out of this mess."
- "I love the Lord, but I don't see how I can find time to serve Him."
- "I know God can make a way, but I'm fed up with my job!"

How can we expect God's blessings when we are torn between two opposites?

The God of this universe spoke words and created the world. He also put creative power in *our* words.

- **Speak faith:** *"I assure you that you can say to this mountain, 'May God lift you up and throw you into the sea,' and your command will be obeyed. All that's required is that you really* *believe and do not doubt in your heart"* (Mark 11:23).

- **Speak creation:** *"Thou shalt also decree a thing, and it shall be established unto thee"* (Job 22:28 KJV).
- **Speak health:** *"Reckless words pierce like a sword, but the tongue of the wise brings healing"* (Proverbs 12:18 NIV).
- **Speak life:** *"The mouth of a righteous man is a well of life"* (Proverbs 10:11 KJV).
- **Speak deliverance:** *"The words of the wicked lie in wait for blood, but the mouth of the upright shall deliver them"* (Proverbs 12:6 AMP).

What flows out of your mouth dictates your future—whether it is positive or negative. Are you confessing God's will?

———◆———

TWO VOICES

DON'T THINK IT STRANGE WHEN YOU HEAR VOICES IN YOUR HEAD—IT HAPPENS TO ALL OF US!

Don't think it strange when you hear voices in your head—it happens to all of us!

You're getting ready for a job interview. One inner voice says, "Relax! You were made for this assignment." The other warns, "Why waste your time? Other applicants will be far better qualified."

The question is, whose report are you going to

believe? And to which voice will you give life by
repeating it out loud?

IT'S YOUR WORDS THAT COUNT

I've met people who are always looking for "a word
from heaven"—anxious for a fellow-believer to prophesy
a blessing over them.

This may come as a surprise to some, but God doesn't
promise to bless anybody else's words over your life. If
they *do* speak, it only becomes effective when you take
what has been said and declare it *yourself.* They must
become *your* words.

Let me explain. As a minister I can pray the sinner's
prayer for you: "Lord, Bill confesses You as Savior and
asks You to come into his heart.

Those are my words, but what about yours?

This prayer must come from your soul and be spoken
to God by *you.* Only then does the blood of Christ cover
your sin and cleanse you from all unrighteousness.

Read these verses carefully: *"Salvation that comes
from trusting Christ—which is the message we preach—
is already within easy reach. In fact, the Scriptures say,
'The message is close at hand; it is on your lips and in
your heart.' For if you confess with your mouth that
Jesus is Lord and believe in your heart that God raised
him from the dead, you will be saved"* (Romans 10:8-9).

The born again experience involves an agreement

between believing and confessing. The moment God sees what is coming out of your mouth reflects the contents of your heart, your salvation is assured.

FUTURE-TALK

To those who don't know God's Word, confession is a rather negative term. They associate it with "I did it. I was wrong. I'm guilty."

Even some religions have "confessionals" as part of their spiritual practices: "Father forgive me for I have sinned."

The danger of such a view is that it can cause you to live your life backwards—looking at your failures instead of your promise.

Why spend any more time on what God has forgiven and forgotten? Remember, your mouth is going to predict your future.

IF THOSE YOU CONVERSE WITH ONLY WANT TO SPEAK ABOUT YOUR PAST, YOU MIGHT CONSIDER EXPANDING YOUR CIRCLE OF FRIENDS!

Start speaking in terms of where the Lord is *now*, and where He desires to take you. Say, "Thank You, Lord, for your plan for my life which gives me hope for the future."

If those you converse with only want to speak about your past, you might consider expanding your circle of friends!

"LET THERE BE..."

Your success is no coincidence and isn't simply the result of a positive mental attitude. It's much more. God created you with power in your words to defeat any negative force.

Let's look back to the dawn of time. *"In the beginning God created the heavens and the earth. The earth*

———◆———
YOUR SUCCESS IS NO COINCIDENCE AND ISN'T SIMPLY THE RESULT OF A POSITIVE MENTAL ATTITUDE.

was empty, a formless mass cloaked in darkness. And the Spirit of God was hovering over its surface. Then God said, 'Let there be light,' and there was light" (Genesis 1:1-3).

The word "let" is only used when there is an opposing force involved. For example, if you were picking up your child from elementary school and saw two bullies taunting him, or beating him up, you wouldn't stand quietly by. You'd shout, "Let him go!"

The reason you say "let" is because something has come against you or those you love—and you want it released.

This is why it is so important to speak words over your household: "Let there be happiness in this marriage." "Let there be peace in this home." "Let there be financial blessing in this place."

You see, when you know the Lord, the forces of the

devil and his demons are diametrically opposed to you—fighting against every blessing you receive from God.

"Let" is a command. You're saying, "Lord, make it happen now!" You are bringing God's power into the situation.

A DISCOURAGING WORD

God doesn't play games! When the children of Israel were headed for the Promised Land, Moses sent twelve spies to check out Canaan. They found a land flowing with milk and honey, yet ten returned with a fearful report. They said, *"We can't go up against them! They are stronger than we are!"* (Numbers 13:31).

So they spread discouraging reports among the Israelites: *"The land we explored will swallow up any who go to live there. All the people we saw were huge. We even saw giants there, the descendants of Anak. We felt like grasshoppers next to them, and that's what we looked like to them!"* (vv. 22-23).

Only two of the spies—Joshua and Caleb—gave an encouraging account when they stood before Moses and the camp: *"Let's go at once to take the land...We can certainly conquer it!"* (v.26).

Who did the people listen to? Those nay-sayers!

"WILL THEY NEVER BELIEVE ME?"

The Bible describes how the entire assembly began to

grumble: *"Their voices rose in a great chorus of complaint against Moses and Aaron. 'We wish we had died in Egypt, or even here in the wilderness!' they wailed. 'Why is the Lord taking us to this country only to have us die in battle? Our wives and little ones will be carried off as slaves! Let's get out of here and return to Egypt!' Then they plotted among themselves, 'Let's choose a leader and go back to Egypt!'"* (Numbers 14:2-4).

———— ◆ ————

MOSES WASN'T THE ONLY ONE TO HEAR THOSE ANGRY WORDS —GOD WAS ALSO LISTENING!

Moses wasn't the only one to hear those angry words—God was also listening!

The Lord said to His chosen leader, *"How long will these people reject me? Will they never believe me, even after all the miraculous signs I have done among them? I will disown them and destroy them with a plague. Then I will make you into a nation far greater and mightier than they are!"* (vv.11-12).

WORDS SEAL YOUR FATE

The Israelites had done nothing *physically*, but their words were contrary to what Jehovah had spoken. What was the consequence? God's hammer of justice fell. Those responsible for spreading negativity were *"struck down and died in a plague"* (Numbers 14:37 NIV).

The rest of the complainers died in the sweltering

desert. An entire generation was wiped out because they spoke against God's promise.

Only two of the spies and their descendants made it to the Promised Land—Joshua and Caleb.

There's a powerful lesson here. God is more patient with negative behavior than He is with negative talk.

Some say, "Well, I read my Bible, go to church and sing in the choir." That may be true, but their unchecked mouth may be destroying their home.

> ◆
>
> GOD IS MORE PATIENT WITH NEGATIVE BEHAVIOR THAN HE IS WITH NEGATIVE TALK.

It's not the conduct, but the communication which is the culprit. Words are determining their fate.

THE DANGER OF "MURMURING"

When you were a child and your parents asked, "Take out the trash," were you obedient, or did you grumble under your breath, "Why do I have to do this? My allowance ought to be more if have to mess with this garbage!"

Later in life your supervisor calls you on your day off with an emergency: "Here's what we need you to do today."

Again, you start to seethe, thinking, "Who does she think she is— interrupting my leisure time!"

Your supervisor may not have heard your words, but

God did. He sees your murmuring spirit.

To *murmur* means "to complain in a low mumbling tone." Remember, that's exactly what the children of Israel did—and the Lord heard every word. He told Moses, *"How long shall I bear with this evil congregation, which murmur against me? I have heard the murmurings of the children of Israel, which they murmur against me. Say unto them, As truly as I live, saith the Lord, as ye have spoken in mine ears, so will I do to you."* (Numbers 14:27-28).

For this offense, they died in the wilderness.

A LIFE-CHANGING CONFESSION

Doesn't it make sense to speak life instead of death?

———◆———

SHE HAD SOMETHING INCREDIBLY POWERFUL—A POSITIVE CONFESSION.

A woman who had suffered with an incurable blood disease for twelve years came to Jesus when He visited her village. Not only was she on the verge of dying, she was financially destitute and lonely.

It would have been so easy for this woman to complain, "I'm poor. No one wants to be my friend because of my disease, and I am going to die!"

Instead, she had something incredibly powerful—a positive confession.

Here are the words she spoke to herself: *"If I could*

only touch his cloak, I will be healed" (Matthew 9:21 NIV). Now everything changed!

Jesus turned around to her and said: *"Daughter, be encouraged! Your faith has made you well"* (v.22). The woman was healed instantly.

I'm not sure whether she received what she confessed or confessed what she received. It makes no difference; a miracle took place.

IT'S NOT OVER!

There is power in speaking over your future.

Before Jesus was crucified, at His trial in front of the religious leaders of the day, the Sanhedrin, people recalled hearing Jesus say, *"I will destroy this Temple made with human hands, and in three days I will build another, made without human hands"* (Mark 14:58).

> I'M NOT SURE WHETHER SHE RECEIVED WHAT SHE CONFESSED OR CONFESSED WHAT SHE RECEIVED. IT MAKES NO DIFFERENCE; A MIRACLE TOOK PLACE.

That should have been a signal to His disciples. He was letting Peter, James and John know: "Don't be dismayed over my death. Just wait. I'm going to meet you over in Galilee!"

Jesus was professing that which had not yet happened.

TANGIBLE RESULTS

Perhaps you have been told, "Don't tell anyone your goal or objective, because if it doesn't happen you'll look foolish."

Remember, the Lord doesn't give power to your secrets, rather to your *words*. Why, because we take a risk—exercising our faith by envisioning tangible results before they occur. Aren't you glad to serve a God who *"gives life to the dead and calls things that are not as though they were"* (Romans 4:17)?

LET THE SEED GROW

Today, begin to speak what you *believe* instead of what you see—what you have experienced or what others are saying.

> ❖
>
> TODAY, BEGIN TO SPEAK WHAT YOU BELIEVE INSTEAD OF WHAT YOU SEE—WHAT YOU HAVE EXPERIENCED, NOT WHAT OTHERS ARE SAYING.

When the Lord gives you a new vocabulary your own words will surprise you. No longer are you talking *down* regarding your relationships or finances. Your speech is now positive and upbeat, because the seed of God's Word is beginning to grow inside—and the signs of spiritual maturity are evident.

90

You declare with confidence:

- "I can do what God says I can do."
- "I can have what God says I can have."
- "I can be what God says I can be."

The day you truly begin to go *all out* is when God's Word is *all in! "...for out of the abundance of the heart the mouth speaketh"* (Matthew 12:34 KJV).

CHAPTER 7

WHAT'S YOUR EQ?

On a scale of 1 to 100, what's your EQ—your Enthusiasm Quotient?

Is your life brimming with passion and excitement, or are you bored, sitting on the sidelines?

Psychologist William Marston asked 3,000 people this question: "What do you have to live for?"

Ninety-four percent responded they were merely enduring their lives, hoping someday things would improve. There was no exuberance, zero "gusto" for living.

Norman Vincent Peale observed: "Years wrinkle the skin, but lack of enthusiasm wrinkles the soul."

SATAN'S FAVORITE WEAPON

The minute you lapse into an "I don't care" attitude, you're playing right into Satan's plan.

A newspaper reporter secured an interview with the

devil. The journalist was especially interested in the deceptive techniques Satan uses to build his reputation."

"What is the most effective tool you use on people?" the reporter asked. "Is it dishonesty? Lust? Jealously?"

"No, no," chuckled the devil. "The best weapon I possess is *apathy*."

It's a technique Satan is still inflicting.

A NEW DIRECTION

I'll never forget the afternoon I was sitting on the steps of a church in Fort Worth, Texas, at the age of 16.

Four years earlier I had given my heart to the Lord—not just as a fire escape from hell, but with the blessed assurance Christ had forgiven my sin.

On those steps, with no one else around, God began dealing with me in a most unusual way. There were no bells ringing or whistles blowing, yet without question the Lord was calling me into full time ministry. Suddenly I knew—beyond a shadow of a doubt—what I was going to do with the rest of my life!

Right there, with the sun beating down, I told the Lord, "I will serve You with every ounce of my being. I give myself to You—there isn't anything I would rather do."

I wasn't sure people would understand. After all, even at that young age, it was assumed I would eventually take over my father's business, or start one of my own.

Now my future was headed in a new direction. To be honest, as a teenager it scared me to death to think of preaching or pastoring a church. Yet, I boldly told the Lord, "I'll serve you wherever You need me." At the time I thought it would be in children's ministry, administrative work, or perhaps to someday assist a minister.

How Could I Keep Silent?

By yielding to God's call, my relationship with Him grew deeper and more powerful—eventually encompassing every area of my life.

As I grew up in church, I drove the leaders crazy because I would challenge their traditionalism. I wanted to know, "How can a person be saved and not be excited about serving the Lord?"

> "How Can a Person Be Saved and Not Be Excited About Serving the Lord?"

If I had things right, when Christ died on the cross:

- He was thinking about my salvation.
- He wanted me to be empowered with the Holy Spirit.
- He was planning for me to spend eternity with Him in heaven.

How could I keep silent about such a Savior? I felt like these words in the Old Testament: *"I am pent up and full of words, and the spirit within me urges me on. I am like a wine cask without a vent. My words are ready to burst out!"* (Job 32:18,19).

BLOWING THE STORM AWAY

No longer did I need to fear death, hell and the grave because those things would no longer have dominion over me. I knew that if I were to die, I would be in the presence of Almighty God.

Even more, the Lord had given me the power to experience a great life on earth.

HE IS THERE TO BLOW THE STORM AWAY, REASSURING ME, "THIS ISN'T GOING TO LAST, HOOPER!"

When I look back, it's my Savior who has protected me all these years. He's the one I can talk to in the middle of the night and feel His presence. If I am hurting or feel betrayed, I know He is there to blow the storm away, reassuring me, "This isn't going to last, Hooper!"

So I have always questioned, "How can people have their lives transformed and not be absolutely thrilled and overjoyed?"

TELL THE WORLD!

You say, "Well, the church we attend is a little more

traditional. We just don't express ourselves too openly."

I'm not talking about your denominational background; if you have found Christ don't you want the world to know?"

If I discovered a cure for cancer or AIDS I would be shouting my discovery to anyone who would listen!

When you stop to think about it, the church is the only institution which deals with a person's eternal life. Since we have the answer—a personal relationship with Jesus Christ—how can we remain silent?

> *IT AMAZES ME BELIEVERS DON'T INVITE THEIR NEIGHBORS TO CHURCH OR LOOK FOR OPPORTUNITIES TO SHARE CHRIST.*

It amazes me believers don't invite their neighbors to church or look for opportunities to share Christ. In every direction there are people with desperate spiritual needs, yet we are reluctant to offer them the real answer.

A FORWARD-MOVING GOD

I have also wondered how church members can come together for a worship service and seem so bored and disinterested. When I think what the Lord has done for me, I can't be complacent; I've got to praise Him—singing a new song to my Savior.

I am convinced the reason so many congregations are stagnant or on life-support is because they are more

97

interested in ritual and tradition than being in touch with a living, breathing, forward-moving God.

The more He does for me, the more I talk about it. Our relationship is ongoing—it's alive!

"ROCK ON!"

Read God's Word and you see how He longs to favor and bless His people. The Bible says, *"For the eyes of the Lord run to and fro throughout the whole earth, to show himself strong in the behalf of them whose heart is perfect toward him"* (2 Chronicles 16:9).

———❖———

WHEN I SMILE AND TELL PEOPLE, "ROCK ON!" I'M REALLY SAYING, "GO WITH GOD'S FAVOR!"

God is not searching for knowledge since He is omniscient. He's not looking for gold—the very streets of heaven are paved with it. Instead, the Lord is searching for someone with a heart for Him.

In the Old Testament the Hebrew word for favor is *roccon*. When I smile and tell people, "Rock on!" I'm really saying, "Go with God's favor!"

LEAPING AND PRAISING!

When the Lord does something marvelous for you, don't just sit there!

Peter, who saw a crippled man begging at the gate, said, *"I don't have any money for you. But I'll give you* what I have. *In the name of Jesus Christ of Nazareth, get up and walk!"* (Acts 3:6). Instantly, the man was healed.

Did he quietly thank Peter and go his merry way? Not at all—this fellow got excited! The Bible records, *"And he leaping up stood, and walked, and entered with them into the temple, walking, and leaping, and praising God"* (v.8).

He asked for alms and received legs!

A MOTIVATED MASTER

There was nothing somber or dull about Jesus. Everywhere He went, people were drawn to Him and came alive. Why? Because He walked this earth with a divine purpose. *"For I have come down from heaven to do the will of God who sent me, not to do what I want"* John 6:38).

Jesus was motivated by compassion.

> ◆
> **THERE WAS NOTHING SOMBER OR DULL ABOUT JESUS. EVERYWHERE HE WENT, PEOPLE WERE DRAWN TO HIM AND CAME ALIVE.**

After hearing the tragic news of the beheading of John the Baptist, the Lord went to a remote area by boat to be alone, *"But the crowds heard where he was headed and followed by land from many villages. A vast crowd was there as he stepped from the boat, and he had compassion on them and healed their sick"* (Matthew 14:13-14).

He was also zealous about winning souls, telling us, *"If you try to keep your life for yourself, you will lose it. But if you give up your life for my sake and for the sake of the Good News, you will find true life. And how do you benefit if you gain the whole world but lose your own soul in the process?"* (Mark 8:35-36).

TURNING THE TABLES!

Jesus certainly knew how to shake up the system. On a journey to Jerusalem during the annual Passover celebration, He went to the Temple and saw the merchants selling cattle, sheep, and doves for sacrifices—and he noticed the money changers behind their counters.

> **"GET THESE THINGS OUT OF HERE. DON'T TURN MY FATHER'S HOUSE INTO A MARKETPLACE!"**
> – JOHN 2:16

What was His reaction? The Bible tells us: *"Jesus made a whip from some ropes and chased them all out of the Temple. He drove out the sheep and oxen, scattered the money changers' coins over the floor, and turned over their tables. Then, going over to the people who sold doves, he told them, "Get these things out of here. Don't turn my Father's house into a marketplace!"* (John 2:15-16).

Even facing the agony of Calvary, there was still an inner confidence. *"He was willing to die a shameful death on the cross because of the joy he knew would be his afterward"* (Hebrews 12:2).

ONE SOLITARY LIFE

Is it any wonder Jesus changed history so dramatically? In the words of James Allen Francis:

He was born in an obscure village,
the child of a peasant woman,
He grew up in another obscure village where He
worked in a carpenter shop until He was thirty.
He never wrote a book. He never held an office.
He never went to college.
He never visited a big city.
He never traveled more than two hundred miles
from the place where He was born.
He did none of the things
usually associated with greatness.
He had no credentials but Himself.

He was only thirty three.
His friends ran away. One of them denied Him.
He was turned over to His enemies and
went through the mockery of a trial.
He was nailed to a cross between two thieves.
While dying, His executioners gambled for His
clothing, the only property He had on earth.

When He was dead, He was laid in a borrowed grave through the pity of a friend.

Nineteen centuries have come and gone, and today Jesus is the central figure of the human race and the leader of mankind's progress.
All the armies that have ever marched;
All the navies that have ever sailed;
All the parliaments that have ever sat;
All the kings that ever reigned put together;
Have not affected the life of mankind on earth as powerfully as that one solitary life.

GIVE IT ALL YOU'VE GOT!

You say, "Wow! If I could be remembered for just one-tenth of one percent of what the Lord accomplished, I would die happy!"

Hold on! Jesus Himself declared, *"Verily, verily, I say unto you, He that believeth on me, the works that I do shall he do also; and greater works than these shall he do; because I go unto my Father"* (John 14:12 KJV).

> **THE LORD HAS GREAT EXPECTATIONS AND IS READY FOR YOU TO EMBRACE LIFE WITH EVERY OUNCE OF ENERGY YOU POSSESS.**

The Lord has great expectations and is ready for you to embrace life with every ounce of energy you possess.

And when you're running on empty, He will refill your tank!

Today make an irrevocable covenant with God to give it all you've got—with no bail-out clauses. Then *"serve the Lord enthusiastically"* (Romans 12:11).

CHAPTER 8

THE GREAT TRADE!

Recently, in one of our Sunday morning services, I asked two people in the congregation to stand and help me illustrate a point I was making during my message.

One was a man who had not been attending our church long, and didn't really know me very well. The other was a woman who had been around our family for several years—and the trust factor for her was somewhat higher.

My sermon this particular morning was titled "Trading Up" and I promised both of them, "If you will accept the deal I propose, you'll be much better off."

I also emphasized the trade we would make would be for real—it wasn't a trick or a gimmick. And the decision would be final. "I will own what you give me, and you will own what I give you in return," I assured them.

First, I turned to the gentleman and asked him how much money he had in his wallet. He hesitated for a moment and answered, "About $100." Then he laughed and explained, "I deposited my paycheck, but haven't given this money to my wife yet!"

Then I stuck my hand down into my pocket and rattled some change. With the congregation listening intently, I proposed: "If you will give me your $100, I'll give you what I have in my pocket. And remember I promised you will be better off when the trade is made. I'll give you one minute to think about it."

It all came down to a simple matter of trust. Could he believe me? Was my word my bond? Would I really come through—or was this just some play on words.

The gentleman had a great sense of humor and said, "Well, you might *think* I would be better off with 50 cents than $100."

"That's the risk," I countered.

When he started negotiating a lower amount I interrupted and explained, "It's all or nothing!"

Thinking about the matter too long, he went past the allotted time I had given him to make up his mind, so the deal was off.

"Go For It, Mom!"

I turned to the woman and saw a lovely wristwatch on her arm. "If you give me your watch, you can have the money I have in my pocket," I offered—still rattling what sounded like some loose change.

As she began taking off her watch she explained, just loud enough for three or four rows of people to hear, "My son bought me this for Mother's Day five years ago."

I repeated what this single mom said and the crowd gasped. However, her son, who was sitting beside her egged her on: "Go for it, Mom!"

So she handed me the watch which obviously meant a great deal to her, and I in return gave her 58 cents.

I started to admire the timepiece, talking about how beautiful it was and how much I really appreciated the trade. She just stood their—remembering the pledge I had made.

"THE EXCHANGE HAS BEEN MADE. THE WATCH IS NOW MINE."

Then I turned to her and said, "You know if you sat down right now my promise just wouldn't be fair." She nodded in agreement.

After reminding her the trade was final, I stated, "The exchange has been made. This watch is now mine, so I can do whatever I want with it...and I choose to give it back to you."

The congregation could visibly see the relief on her face.

"And with it" I continued (reaching into my other pocket), "I want to wrap it in these four $100 bills." And I handed the watch back to its rightful owner.

The woman started to cry and her son stood up and

hugged her. It was obvious she needed the money.

When the mom tried to return the cash, people around her began saying, "A deal is a deal!"

You should have seen the look of regret on the face of the man who refused to make the bargain!

It's exactly the same with God. Without trust, you will never be able to "trade up."

TAKE A BITE!

Have you ever known someone who devoted his or her life to the wrong pursuit—content to settle for second best? Perhaps it was a person totally dedicated to a career or even a hobby—something they thought would bring them happiness, satisfaction or success. Yet, their quest left them feeling empty and unfulfilled.

> ◆
> "HOW WOULD YOU LIKE A BITE OF THIS CHOCOLATE BUNNY?"

One Sunday morning about a week before Easter, I stepped off the platform holding a large chocolate Easter bunny in a boxed wrapper. Picking out a nine-year-old boy seated on the first row with his family, I asked, "How would you like a bite of this chocolate bunny?"

His eyes lit up and his head began nodding, "Yes!" He was almost drooling at the prospect.

"Well, get ready for a mouthful of chocolate," I

suggested—setting him up for the treat. I'm sure his tastebuds began working overtime.

Then I proceeded to tell the audience the correct way to eat a chocolate Easter bunny. "You bite the ears off first," I said, smiling.

THAT EMPTY FEELING

The time had come for what this boy was anticipating. He walked up to the front of the church and eagerly took a huge bite out of the ear of the bunny,

What a shock! Instead of a mouthful of solid chocolate, there was only a small fraction of what he expected. The bunny was hollow inside—only a shell.

In life, we all have encountered things we believed would bring pure joy, yet instead left us feeling cheated and empty.

AN ENDLESS SEARCH

If we are willing to give our one-and-only existence to a cause, we'd better make certain the payoff is worth the effort.

Some battles are not worth the fight —and some ladders are not worth the climb. What a waste to live and never experience true, lasting satisfaction.

In the late 1920s William Phelps wrote an extremely popular book, *The Pursuit of Happiness.* Since then, there have been thousands more who have suggested ways we can find inner peace.

The hunt for personal fulfillment is an age-old quest. It should come as no surprise that the first public message of Jesus—the Sermon on the Mount—centered on happiness, and how to live a blessed life. It's referred to as The Beatitudes.

God wants us to be filled with joy and experience our days on this earth to their fullest. In the words of His Son: *"The thief comes only in order to steal and kill and destroy. I came that they may have and enjoy life, and have it in abundance (to the full, till it overflows)"* (John 10:10 AMP).

GOOD MEDICINE

As a pastor I often meet and counsel people who believe God is upset with them—and that He is the reason their life is so dysfunctional. They are misguided, feeling they actually deserve to be unhappy, not realizing the Lord desires only the best for them. God not only wants to make our dreams come true, He delights in our happiness and takes pleasure in our praise.

Start smiling—it's good for you! Medical research has documented that people heal much faster if they are happy. As God's Word tells us: *"A cheerful heart is good medicine"* (Proverbs 17:22).

Doctors have discovered it takes 72 face muscles to

frown and only 14 face muscles to smile. Perhaps the reason there are so many tired people is because their face is wearing them out!

A mother and daughter went shopping together and, unfortunately, the mom was not in a good mood. After constantly complaining about the high prices and slow service received in several stores, they were exiting one department when the agitated mother said, "Did you see the look that salesperson gave me?"

The daughter bluntly replied, "Mother, the salesperson didn't give you that look, you had it when you walked in!"

> ◆
>
> "DID YOU SEE THE LOOK THAT SALESPERSON GAVE ME?"

WHERE IS IT FOUND?

Life is to short to travel road after road, mile after mile, only to face one more dead-end journey. This is why God gave us the Holy Bible—so we can have an understanding of what path to pursue; what works and what doesn't.

From the Word and observing the lives of others, we know:

1. Happiness is not found in circumstances.

I've heard people say, "Oh, if I could just live in another neighborhood, my life would be so much better."

Or, " If I just had more education, I'd have it made!"

Look around and you'll find millions who desperately search for peace, thinking they'll find contentment if they could just be someplace else. It's what Daniel prophesied would happen in the end times when *"many shall rush here and there"* (Daniel 12:4 KJV).

> ◆
> **EXTERNAL CIRCUMSTANCES DON'T PRODUCE HAPPINESS. RATHER, IT IS THE RESULT OF AN INTERNAL DECISION.**

External circumstances don't produce happiness. Rather, it is the result of an internal decision.

The apostle Paul, in his letter to the believers at Philippi, tells them to rejoice—and he said it 14 times!

"Rejoice in the Lord always. I will say it again: Rejoice" (Philippians 4:4 NIV).

What's amazing is this joy-filled book on inner contentment was written while Paul was behind bars in prison!

2. Happiness is not found in money.

Those who think more money will solve their problems are only deluding themselves. One study reported Americans represent 5% percent of the world's population, own 60% of its wealth, yet consume 90% of all the tranquilizers being manufactured.

If wealth brings happiness, why do so many of the super-rich engage in such self-destructive behavior?

One multi-millionaire businessman—who could own anything money can buy—said before his death, "I suppose I'm the most miserable person on the planet."

What is God's opinion on the matter? *"Those who love money will never have enough. How absurd to think that wealth brings true happiness!"* (Ecclesiastes 5:10).

It's a principle we all must learn.

3. Happiness is not found in fame.

Those who believe celebrity status automatically brings lasting contentment haven't been paying attention. Just look at the tragic demise of Janis Joplin, Jimi Hendrix and John Belushi, to name just a few.

Shortly after the suicide of rock star Curt Cobain, a reporter for MTV was asked, if she knew of any other famous person who was in danger of taking his or her own life. She responded, "I don't know of any who *are* not candidates for suicide, because I can't name one who is truly happy."

What an indictment!

The formula for happiness is found throughout God's Word, but here's a verse that states it exactly: *"In thy presence is fullness of joy, at thy right hand there are pleasures for evermore"* (Psalm 16:11 KJV).

A FINAL QUEST

Solomon is credited for writing three books of the Bible: (1) The Song of Solomon (which is believed to have been written when he was a younger man), (2) Proverbs (scribed when Solomon was in his mid-life), and (3) Ecclesiastes (written toward the end of his days).

In the second chapter of Ecclesiastes, Solomon launches one final search to uncover what life is all about. Here, diligently searching for answers, was the wisest person on the planet—and wealthy enough to afford this adventure to "try it all."

In the first ten verses of chapter two, Solomon lists some of his pursuits while trying to find meaning and happiness. They include: pleasure, wine, foolishness, building huge homes, beautiful gardens and parks, an increase in his number of employees, herds and flocks, investments, money, the arts, women and fame.

He sums up his search with this statement: *"But as I looked at everything I had worked so hard to accomplish, it was all so meaningless. It was like chasing the wind. There was nothing really worthwhile anywhere"* (Ecclesiastes 2:11).

To Solomon, life resembled biting into that hollow Easter bunny!

Fortunately, this wise man found the answer to what truly mattered—and in the process became totally committed to God.

Here are three of Solomon's conclusions:

First: Enjoy your wife and family. *"Live happily with the woman you love through all the meaningless days of life that God has given you in this world. The wife God gives you is your reward for all your earthly toil"* (Ecclesiastes 9:9).

Second: Get a kick out of the work you do every day. *"A man can do nothing better than...find satisfaction in his work"* (Ecclesiastes 2:24 NIV).

Third: Love the Lord and "do life" His way. *"Here is my final conclusion: Fear God and obey his commands"* (Ecclesiastes 12:13).

You and I have been created in the image and likeness of an Almighty God, and true happiness can only be found as a byproduct of a relationship with Him.

Are you willing to exchange your "trivial pursuits" for something that will last for eternity?

It will be the best trade you'll ever make!

CHAPTER 9

LIVE LIKE YOU WERE DYING

I was driving along in my car and pushed the radio button to a country station. A few minutes later, Tim McGraw was singing a song I'd never heard before—"Live Like You Were Dying." It's about a man in his early 40s who has been given the news he doesn't have long to live.

I was riveted to the words—and how this person responded to the doctor's report. One of the lines especially caught my attention: "I loved deeper and I spoke sweeter and I watched an eagle as it was flying."

GOD'S CALENDAR

As I reflected on the song, I thought, "This is what the Lord asks of each of us—to live like we are dying—because we are! The mortality rate in the U.S. is

100 percent!

Long ago, King Solomon made this observation:

"There is a time for everything,
a season for every activity under heaven.
A time to be born and a time to die.
A time to plant and a time to harvest.
A time to kill and a time to heal.
A time to tear down and a time to rebuild.
A time to cry and a time to laugh.
A time to grieve and a time to dance.
A time to scatter stones and a time to gather
stones.
A time to embrace and a time to turn away.
A time to search and a time to lose.
A time to keep and a time to throw away.
A time to tear and a time to mend.
A time to be quiet and a time to speak up.
A time to love and a time to hate.
A time for war and a time for peace"
(Ecclesiastes 3:1-8)

THE CHANGES I WOULD MAKE

When I was young it seemed that Christmas would never arrive, but the older I become the faster the seasons fly by. Life is short and eternity is long. That's why the Bible says: *"Teach us to number our days and recognize how few they are; help us to spend them as we should"* (Psalm 90:12).

Knowing God keeps a schedule book for each of His children, I began to ask myself, "Dan, what changes would you make if you knew this week—or this month—would be your last?"

> *"What Changes Would You Make if You Knew This Week—or This Month—Would Be Your Last?"*

Here is my list:

1. I would refuse to argue about petty issues.

We allow ourselves to become animated and agitated over minutia—things that don't really matter. And we bicker over topics which five years from today are just blips on our radar screen.

The Bible counsels: *"Don't have anything to do with foolish and stupid arguments, because you know they produce quarrels. And the Lord's servant must not quarrel; instead, he must be kind to everyone, able to teach, not resentful"* (2 Timothy 2:23-24 NIV).

2. I would be kinder and more understanding of those around me.

If you dropped every friendship with those who fail to live up to your expectations, you would probably be without any friends!

119

Jesus tells us to look introspectively—then we won't be so judgmental of others. He asks: *"...why worry about a speck in your friend's eye when you have a log in your own? How can you think of saying, 'Let me help you get rid of that speck in your eye,' when you can't see past the log in your own eye? Hypocrite! First get rid of the log from your own eye; then perhaps you will see well enough to deal with the speck in your friend's eye"* (Matthew 7:3-5).

3. I would refuse to respond to offenses.

Why waste valuable time on "mean-spirited" people who delight in irritating and upsetting you? Regardless of the garbage they throw your way, make a decision you will rise above it.

I heard about a farmer's donkey that tragically fell into a deep, unused well.

The animal cried pitifully for hours as the frantic farmer tried to figure out what to do. Finally he decided the animal was old and the well needed to be covered up anyway, so it just wasn't worth the effort to try and rescue the donkey.

He invited all his neighbors to come over and help him with his solution. They each grabbed a shovel and began to throw dirt into the well.

At first, the frightened donkey realized what was happening and brayed loudly. Then, to everyone's surprise, he quieted down. A few shovel loads later, the farmer looked down the well and was astonished at what he saw.

With every pile of dirt that hit his back, the donkey was doing something unbelievable. He would shake it off and take a step up. As the farmer's neighbors continued to throw dirt on top of the trapped animal, he would shake it off and take a step up.

Pretty soon, everyone gasped as the donkey stepped up over the edge of the well and trotted off!

This story may be a little far-fetched, but life is going to treat you the same, covering you with piles of dirt.

The trick to surviving is to emulate the donkey. Shake it off and take a step up. Each of our troubles represent a stepping stone. We can free ourselves by never quitting.

> ◆
>
> **EACH OF OUR TROUBLES REPRESENT A STEPPING STONE.**

Remember: shake it off, and take a step up!

As a believer, how should you react when people innocently or maliciously wound you with their words? If you stay centered on God's Word, it reacts like Teflon—nothing sticks. As the psalmist writes: *"Great peace have they which love thy law: and nothing shall offend them"* (Psalm 119:165 KJV).

4. I would make sure I would see my family again in heaven.

Never take the salvation of those we love lightly or

for granted. There comes a time when we need to have some face-to-face, heart-to-heart conversations with our relatives concerning their faith—and their eternal destiny.

If you have members of your family who don't understand their need for repentance, you are not alone. Even Jesus had a difficult time reaching His loved ones.

Scripture records what happened after the Lord launched His public ministry and began to cast out devils: *"When his family heard what was happening, they tried to take him home with them. 'He's out of his mind,' they said"* (Mark 3:21). We also learn that *"even his brothers didn't believe in him"* (John 7:5).

Yet, Jesus demonstrated His faith and eventually won His family. After the resurrection, we find Mary at a prayer meeting (Acts 1:14) and His brother, James, a "pillar" of the church (Galatians 2:9).

If you are praying for the conversion of your family, claim the words Paul and Silas spoke to the Philippian jailer, who asked, "What must I do to be saved?" They replied, *"Believe on the Lord Jesus and you will be saved, along with your entire household"* (Acts 16:31).

That's a promise for you!

5. I would say the things we usually reserve for when someone is gone.

Why do so many wait for a funeral service to express their deep affection and respect for a loved one? Can you imagine how elated they would feel if you poured out your heart while they were still alive?

Today, take a drive or pick up the phone and tell your mom, dad, brother, sister, son or daughter, "I just want you to know how proud I am of you and how much I love you."

6. I would create memories and leave a legacy.

I've never seen a hearse pulling a U-Haul!

The real treasures of life are not the size of your bank account or the material possessions you accumulate. You can't take those with you.

Instead, make a commitment to leave a heritage that truly lasts—a lifetime of God-centered memories your family will cherish forever. What will be remembered? A walk in the park, a bedtime prayer, singing Christmas carols with your kids, or a simple squeeze of the hand. These have value beyond measure.

I'VE NEVER SEEN A HEARSE PULLING A U-HAUL!

Express your feelings with the same transparency Paul wrote in his letter to the believers at Thessalonica: *"But Timothy has just now come to us from you and has brought good news about your faith and love. He has told us that you always have pleasant memories of us and that you long to see us, just as we also long to see you"* (1 Thessalonians 3:6).

123

7. I would make sure I'm saved.

Over the years, I've asked this question more times than I can count, "Have you accepted Christ as your personal Savior?"

The variety of answers continue to amaze me:

- "Well, I was *baptized* when I was a baby."
- "I've been trying to serve the church for all of my adult life."
- "I'm a pretty good person who believes in God."

You can't dance around or skirt the issue. Salvation is not the result of just believing there *is* a God, but asking His Son to forgive your sin and cleanse you from all unrighteousness.

———◆——— **YOU CAN'T DANCE AROUND OR SKIRT THE ISSUE.**

Nicodemus, a member of the Jewish ruling council, was told by Jesus that in order to see the Kingdom of God, *"You must be born again"* (John 3:7 NIV).

The man was confused, asking, *"How can a man be born when he is old?...Surely he cannot enter a second time into his mother's womb to be born"* (v.4 NIV).

Jesus explained it was a spiritual birth: *"For God so*

loved the world that he gave his only Son, so that everyone who believes in him will not perish but have eternal life" (v.16).

Have you—from the depths of your heart—asked Christ to cleanse you with His precious blood? He's waiting to hear your prayer and make you a new creation!

> **HAVE YOU—FROM THE DEPTHS OF YOUR HEART—ASKED CHRIST TO CLEANSE YOU WITH HIS PRECIOUS BLOOD?**

8. I would be looking for my Savior.

Early one morning, a young boy about 10 years old was standing in the middle of the block with his backpack full of books.

A man who lived nearby went out to retrieve his newspaper and, concerned, asked the lad what he was doing. The youngster replied, "I'm waiting on the school bus."

"Well, it doesn't stop here in the middle of the block," the man said emphatically. "You will need to walk down the street to the bus stop."

"Oh, I know it will stop right here" replied the boy.

The man insisted, "It doesn't matter what you believe, that bus isn't going to stop."

Just then a big yellow school bus turned the corner, pulled up in front of the boy, hit the brakes and opened the door.

As the young lad started to climb into the bus, he looked back at the neighbor, shrugged his shoulders, grinned and proudly announced, "The bus driver is my dad!"

Friend, you have a Heavenly Father who is not going to leave you stranded on the side of the road. The Lord knows where you are and you won't be forgotten. He says, *"Never will I leave you; never will I forsake you"* (Hebrews 13:5 NIV).

One day soon, Christ will return to take His children home. The Bible declares, *"For the Lord himself shall descend from heaven with a shout, with the voice of the archangel, and with the trump of God: and the dead in Christ shall rise first: Then we which are alive and remain shall be caught up together with them in the clouds, to meet the Lord in the air: and so shall we ever be with the Lord"* (1 Thessalonians 4:16-17 KJV).

I can hardly wait!

THE COUNTDOWN HAS BEGUN FOR WHAT WILL BE THE MOST STARTLING EVENT IN HUMAN HISTORY—THE RAPTURE OF THE CHURCH.

GET READY!

The countdown has begun for what will be the most startling event in human history—the rapture of the church. If you know Christ, this is not a time for fear, but one of joy. Paul described it as the *"blessed hope"* (Titus 2:13).

We cannot avoid this fact: *"...it is appointed unto men once to die, but after this the judgment"* (Hebrews 9:27 KJV). At that great moment, I look forward to hearing the Lord say, "Well done!"

Have you made preparations for tomorrow? It will change the way you live today!

CHAPTER 10

JUST FINISH IT!

I was only seven years old when I had my first job—helping my father in his furniture business he had owned for over 46 years.

The 25 cents-an-hour pay he gave me was probably just to stay out of his way, even though he knew how much I loved being around him.

One day while Dad was working on a kitchen cabinet door with a power sander I said, "I want to learn how to use that thing." Up to this point I was only given a little block of wood with a piece of sandpaper wrapped around it.

He thought for a moment, then replied, "Well, I'll be happy to show you how to use a power sander, but there is one thing you have to promise me."

"What's that?" I asked.

"If you start sanding a door you have to finish it. I'm not going to complete the project for you. You have got to do it all yourself."

QUITTING WASN'T AN OPTION

Dad wasn't kidding—it was an invaluable lesson he also instilled in my two brothers and sister. "You can do anything you want, just make sure you finish what you start," he wisely told us.

We could sign up for any sport, from swimming to karate, but dropping out before the final game or lesson was out of the question. Why? Because my father knew life was full of challenges, and only those who persevered and hung in there survived.

———◆———

"YOU CAN DO ANYTHING YOU WANT, JUST MAKE SURE YOU FINISH WHAT YOU START."

One of the great legacies Dad left was the time he was willing to invest in each of his children.

I still remember the day my father and my older brother, Mark, were under the car in our driveway, dropping the engine out so they could rework it.

As I walked by, my dad asked, "Son, do you want to crawl under here and learn how an engine works?"

"No thanks," I quickly responded—knowing if I climbed underneath that car I wasn't coming out until the job was finished. It was too much information for me.

To this day I have no idea how an automobile works!

"MISSION ACCOMPLISHED"

The monuments of great world leaders are not erected to honor those who *began* a task, rather those who completed their work.

This basic principle of life is also found in scripture:

- **God completed His creation:** *"On the seventh day, having finished his task, God rested from all his work"* (Genesis 2:2).
- **Solomon finished the Temple:** He *"made sure that all the work related to building the Temple of the Lord was carried out, from the day its foundation was laid to the day of its completion"* (2 Chronicles 8:16).
- **Paul desired a "Mission Accomplished":** *"Now you should carry this project through to completion just as enthusiastically as you began it"* (2 Corinthians 8:11).
- **Jesus had one major objective:** It was *"to do the will of him who sent me and to finish his work"* (John 4:34 NIV).

"CARRY YOUR CROSS"

Many give up because they fail to accurately count the cost of achievement.

This happens to students who find out the night before a major exam the incredible amount of study

131

required to pass a course. We also see it in business when an entrepreneur fails to set aside the cash-flow needs of a startup enterprise.

Read the history of military warfare and you'll find a record of armies who have been forced to wave the white flag because they were not prepared for the conflict.

When Jesus chose the disciples, He warned them in advance the journey would be arduous—and enormous sacrifice would be required: *"And you cannot be my disciples if you do not carry your own cross and follow me"* (Luke 14:27).

Jesus continued: *"But don't begin until you count the cost. For who would begin construction of a building without first getting estimates and then checking to see if there is enough money to pay the bills. Otherwise you might complete only the foundation before running out of the funds and then how everyone would laugh at you. They would say, there is the person that started that building and ran out of money before it was finished. Or what king would ever dream of going to war without first sitting down with his counselors and discussing whether his army of 10,000 is strong enough to defeat the 20,000 soldiers who are marching against him. If he is not able then while the enemy is still far away he will send a delegation to discuss terms of peace. So no one can become my disciple without giving up everything first"* (vv.28-33).

The bottom line is: never pick a fight you don't plan to finish.

A "NOW" REWARD

Some lose heart and become discouraged when they realize they can't be a true follower of Christ without "giving up everything first."

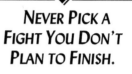

NEVER PICK A FIGHT YOU DON'T PLAN TO FINISH.

However, when we willingly surrender ourselves to the Lord, it's just the beginning of His great abundance. Jesus tells us: *"I assure you that everyone who has given up house or brothers or sisters or mother or father or children or property, for my sake and for the Good News, will receive now in return, a hundred times over"* (Mark 10:29-30).

Yes, we will be rewarded for our sacrifice in the world to come—but also *now!*

YOU ARE SAFE!

Skeptics wonder, "How could a loving God even ask us to give up our brothers, sisters and parents for His cause?"

It's a spiritual matter. Jesus is saying you cannot *allow* any relationship to take precedence over Him.

For example, if your affection is attached more to your parents than to Christ, the enemy turns this against you—perhaps using your parents to break your heart.

133

The same is true if your number one priority is your spouse, a child, a friendship or your job. Satan will manipulate these attachments to tear you apart.

However, if your faith and confidence is in Christ, there is nothing Satan can use against you. You are safe!

STAY PLANTED

I've met people who have a "quitting spirit." For some, this has been inherited through the generations. Looking back, they realize their mom, dad and grandparents demonstrated a pattern of faltering and giving up when things grew tough. They recklessly abandoned relationships, didn't finish their education, or threw in the towel while building a business.

One small argument and all of a sudden an angry couple is talking divorce—thinking the grass is greener on the other side of the fence. Whoa! Are they in for a shock!

This syndrome also happens in church. A member ruffles the feathers of a fellow attender and the offended party heads for the door—looking for another congregation.

Please understand, we can't keep ripping roots out of the ground and still expect a harvest. It's only when we *remain* planted—deepening our roots—that we grow and prosper.

STEP BY STEP

The next time someone says, "You're really a piece of work," thank them for the compliment!

That statement is true. You are at a certain stage of a major project you will finish in *phases*. It takes time, planning and patience.

◆

DAVID DIDN'T DEFEAT GOLIATH IN A SPLIT SECOND; THERE WERE NUMEROUS STEPS INVOLVED.

David didn't defeat Goliath in a split second; there were numerous steps involved:

1. **He prepared for battle:** David *"picked up five smooth stones from a stream and put them in his shepherd's bag. Then, armed only with his shepherd's staff and sling, he started across to fight Goliath"* (1 Samuel 17:40).

2. **He confronted the giant:** David shouted to the Philistine, *"You come to me with sword, spear, and javelin, but I come to you in the name of the Lord Almighty—the God of the armies of Israel, whom you have defied"* (v.45).

3. **He charged forward**: *"As Goliath moved closer to attack, David quickly ran out to meet him"* (v.48).

4. **He launched the assault:** *"Reaching into his shepherd's bag and taking out a stone, he hurled it from his sling and hit the Philistine in*

135

the forehead. The stone sank in, and Goliath stumbled and fell face downward to the ground" (v.49).

5. **He finished the task:** *The shepherd boy "ran over and pulled Goliath's sword from its sheath. David used it to kill the giant and cut off his head"* (v.51).

There was jubilation in Israel!

"THAT'S GOOD!"

Believe me, before any celebration there's plenty of work to be done. As we learn in the life of David, it's the small victories along the way that release creative power—allowing us to progress to the next step and function ever better.

---❖---

THE GIANT SOME PEOPLE GRAPPLE WITH CAN BE SEEN RIGHT IN THEIR OWN MIRROR.

The giant some people grapple with can be seen right in their own mirror. For example, there are overweight individuals who desperately need to lose as much as 100 pounds.

How is this feat accomplished? Rather than going for the "whole enchilada" you set a series of small goals and rejoice at every milestone. I'm not recommending you over-indulge with a Big Mac and an order of super-sized fries.

No. When you lose ten pounds, say "Thank You, Lord for giving me will power"—then go for the next ten!

God gave us the example. He created the earth in five days, and in five phases. First He separated light from darkness, then divided the water from land. Next He created vegetation, then seasons and animal life. After each day He looked down at what He had formed and exclaimed, "That's good!"

On the sixth day, God created man. It wasn't just good—*"and behold it was very good"* (Genesis 1:31 KJV). This was an event worthy of excitement!

Celebrate!

I'm convinced there are many who would like to celebrate, yet they are surrounded by individuals who don't understand the principle. They are lightning-quick to remind you of what you "didn't" do—regardless of your great strides.

Forget these people and mark the special occasion with joy every time you have a chance:

- If you've had difficulty keeping a job, yet you've stayed with your new employer six months – celebrate!
- If you've been a life-long smoker and have successfully gone 60 days without a cigarette—take time to pat yourself on the back!

■ If it's been your goal to read the Bible from cover to cover—have a time of celebration when you complete the book of Revelation!

FINISH THE COURSE

Listen to what the apostle Paul said to young Timothy: *"I have fought a good fight, I have finished my course, I have kept the faith"* (2 Timothy 4:7 KJV).

God has not given you the ability to fulfill my mission; nor has He given me the grace to do yours. We haven't been asked to complete the race of our spouse or our children—it's personal, ours alone!

Paul was an evangelist in his region of the known world, yet not everyone he preached salvation to accepted Christ. Still, he could say, "I have finished my course."

The entire job was not yet completed, but Paul's part was! Remember: *"Finishing is better than starting"* (Ecclesiastes 7:8).

WHAT'S YOUR MISSION?

I'm an eternal optimist who loves to remedy problems—and have always believed "where there is a will there's a way." Until one day I was reading the New Testament and came upon a scripture that startled me. Jesus said, *"You will always have the poor among you"* (Matthew 26:11).

Wow! I suddenly understood there are some issues we will *never* be able to resolve in this life—no matter how hard we try.

To be honest, that verse liberated me. I realized the world wasn't resting on my shoulders.

This doesn't mean we stop trying to change lives. Far from it. God expects us to be salt and light to every person who crosses our path. His mission statement has never altered: *"And he said unto them, Go ye into all the world, and preach the gospel to every creature. He that believeth and is baptized shall be saved; but he that believeth not shall be damned"* (Mark 16:15-16).

No one man can save the entire world. There are those who will believe on Christ, and others who choose to reject the Savior. Our commission is to spread the Word and leave the rest in God's capable hands.

> ◆
> **THE CREATOR DOESN'T INTEND FOR HIS CHILDREN TO MERELY SURVIVE—HE WANTS US TO THRIVE!**

ALPHA AND OMEGA

The Creator doesn't intend for His children to merely survive—He wants us to thrive! For that to happen, we are to finish what He inspires us to start.

It's exhilarating to know we serve a God who is the *"Alpha and Omega, the First and the Last, the Beginning and the End"* (Revelation 22:13).

Our Heavenly Father didn't launch a plan of salvation, then suddenly abandon the idea. No. He sent His only Son to earth—to be born as a Man and to die on a cross—for our sin. Jesus completed what God began; He is the *"author and finisher of our faith"* (Hebrews 12:2 KJV).

Think of it! We only need to accept the work which has already been done. When Christ declared *"It is finished"* (John 19:30 KJV), a brand new chapter in history was opened. For the first time we could know salvation by faith, not by sacrifice.

THE "GOOD WORK"

Christ completed His divine assignment, yet as His children we are still "works in progress"—being shaped and perfected in preparation for eternity.

How does God fulfill His mission? Through born again believers like you and me. We place His will in motion—and are His feet and hands on earth.

God declares: *"The word that goes out of my mouth it will not return to me empty. But will accomplish what I desire and achieve the purpose for which I sent it"* (Isaiah 55:11 NIV).

Again, we need to make this personal. The Father is saying: "If I speak words over you, they will carry out my purpose for your life." Even more, *"He who began a good work in you will carry it on to completion until the day of Jesus Christ"* (Philippians 1:6 NIV).

The Lord initiated something amazing in your life and He plans on finishing it. All He asks of us is: "Don't let Me down. Don't quit on Me now!"

God's Word promises: *"...as thy days, so shall thy strength be"* (Deuteronomy 33:25). This guarantees you'll have Monday's strength for Monday's challenges, new power for Tuesday, and additional power to last until He calls you home.

YOUR "ALL OUT" VOW

This is no time to lose heart and call it quits. The Lord has created, transformed and placed you exactly where you are for His divine purpose.

Today, I pray the message you have just read will burst within your heart—and you will make this vow to the Lord: "I totally surrender all that I am and everything I have. I'm going *all out* for You!"

For a Complete List of Publications
and Media Materials, or to Schedule the
Author for Speaking Engagements,
Contact:

Dan Hooper
Hooper Ministries
765 24 Road
Grand Junction, CO 81505

Phone: 970-245-7729